MILNER CRAFT SERIES

DIANA LAMPE'S

EMBROIDERY

from the garden

SALLY MILNER PUBLISHING

First published in 1997 by
Sally Milner Publishing Pty Ltd
RMB 54 Burra Road
Burra Creek
NSW Australia 2620
Reprinted 1998

Design by Samantha Seery, ANU Graphics, Canberra
Photography by Ben Wrigley and Steve Neubauer, Canberra
Photograph of author by Irene Lorbergs, Canberra
Printed and bound by Impact Printing, Melbourne

Cataloguing-in-Publication data:

Lampe, Diana.
    Embroidery from the garden.

    Bibliography.
    Includes index.
    ISBN 1 86351 206 3

    1. Embroidery—Patterns. 2. Decoration and ornament—
    Plant forms. I. Title.

746.44041

In memory of
Paddy June Hornsby

ACKNOWLEDGMENTS

It is hard to know where to start thanking the many people who have been involved in the production of this book. It would not have happened without Sally Milner, my publisher, and Janet Roche, my South African friend and fellow embroiderer.

Thank you Sally for sending me to South Africa, for your patience and encouragement and for publishing this book. Thank you also to Janet Roche and her charming husband Royden for organising an exciting trip for me and looking after me so well. It was a wonderful experience!

My love and appreciation go to my family, my mother May Lampe and my children, Charlotte, Sophie and Nicholas, who continue to encourage and support me. Sophie has been particularly helpful with the computer. I also wish to thank David Harper for his help and legal advice.

I dedicate this book to Paddy June Hornsby in gratitude for her love and friendship, support and encouragement. My embroidered *Gerbera* and *Rhodohypoxis* were designed in her garden and are my gift to her memory. Her warmth and grace, sense of fun and generosity of spirit continue to influence those who knew her.

Many people have helped me in different ways and I wish to thank them most sincerely for their part in *Embroidery from the Garden*. They include Keith Alden, Dianna Budd, Geoffrey Brooks, Jenny Brennan, Rita Crawford, Neale Emanuel, Dianne Firth, Madge Guthrie, Joan Jackson, Jan Joliffe, Krystyna Koltun,

Samantha Kors, Lynne Harlow, Carolyn Pennington, Emma Pickens, Phillipa Saunders, Maggie Taylor, Bernadette Thomas and Merrilyn Whittle. A special thanks to June Humphrey for finding for me the lovely South African poem *Cosmos* by Francis Ernley Walrond.

Thanks also go to Samantha Seery for the book's design, to Ben Wrigley, Steve Neubauer, and Irene Lorbergs for the splendid photography, Don Bradford for the clear stitch illustrations and Ross Henty for allowing me to reproduce 'The Framing of Needlework'.

I wish to thank Dollfus-Mieg & Cie - Paris, for giving me permission to use the DMC ™ trademark and for donating the threads used in the designs.

Finally I would like to express my appreciation to my students and to all the people who enjoy and promote my work. Their interest and enthusiasm encourage me to keep designing even more embroidered flowers and providing material for another book!

Diana Lampe, 1997

COSMOS

by Francis Ernley Walrond

Bright flowers, of varied tender-tinted hues,
Red, white, and purple-pink,
And lightly poised upon your stems of green,
Like flame upon a candle.
Who would have thought the stern and sombre veld
Could nourish things so delicately fair?
It is as though a man morose and sad,
Whose thoughts are twilight-tinged and grey,
Should suddenly uplift a tuneful voice
And troll a love-song.

For, as some painter with a dream of heaven
May fill his background in with cherub's heads,
Faces of lovely children
With dimpled smiles that only childhood knows,
So Nature, ever seeking new effects,
And tiring of old sameness, here
Has taken children's faces,
And breathing turned them into flowers,
And strewn them laughing o'er the barren veld.
You men of bounded lives,
Whose music is the clicking of the keys,
And all your colour painted scrip,
Leave these in God's name, who made Nature fair,
And for an hour at least,
Gazing upon this loveliness, forget
The buying and selling of the world.
Come forth and view
These regiments of firm-encampèd flowers,
These dancing faces in their sea of green,
And ye shall know,
Unless your hearts be wholly dried
And squeezed of power to love the lovelier things,
A sweeter joy than any walls enclose.

CONTENTS

Chapter 1
Chapter 2
Chapter 3
Chapter 4
Chapter 5
Chapter 6
Chapter 7
Chapter 8

The Strelitzia Garden with flowers

INTRODUCTION

Looking for an inspiration to write this introduction I browsed through two beautiful books which I brought back from South Africa. You may like to read them too. They are: *Namaqualand Garden of the Gods* by Freeman Patterson (Human and Rousseau) and *A Fynbos Year* illustrated by Liz McMahon with text by Michael Fraser (David Philip). Looking at them has made me want to go back to this beautiful country in the Spring.

My trip to South Africa was the realisation of a life-long dream. Whilst on safari in Londolzi I had to pinch myself as a reminder it was real.

The flora of Southern Africa is so rich one could spend a lifetime studying it. For instance there are more species of bulbs found there than anywhere else. It has been endlessly fascinating for me to research and study the flowering plants of this region. Many of them are very beautiful. Examples are the graceful *Dierama pulcherrimum* and the unusual blue *Ixia viridflora*. Others are bright and cheerful such as the daisies and geraniums.

The flowers I have chosen to design in embroidery for this book are well known and commonly grown in Australia and other parts of the world. Some of these plants have been extensively hybridised and as a result have become common throughout the world. Examples are the *Geranium, Gerbera* and *Gladioli.*

I spend a great deal of time collecting different species and growing them in my garden. I have set aside part of my garden specially to grow plants of Southern African origin. Although I live in a temperate climate I find most species to be so hardy they thrive in this climate. Only the tropical species find it too cold.

People who are interested in my work often ask me which comes first the embroidery or the garden. In reply I like to use the analogy of the chicken and the egg. One inspires the other.

I am also asked about the process of designing my embroidered flowers. I like to design a new embroidered flower with a specimen in front of me. This helps me capture the essence of the plant. I carefully match the threads with the plant, sometimes blending different colours in the needle for the required effect. I sketch and photograph the plant as part of the process and to keep as a record.

This book is the end result of three years work. My ambition in writing it has been to document the embroidered designs so other people can enjoy them too. I find studying flowering plants and devising ways to depict them realistically in needlework to be an absorbing pastime. I also enjoy writing the instructions and illustrating the designs.

The individual flowers, described in the Flower Glossary, can be used for many purposes. They can be worked in any size or medium you wish such as silk or wool. You can adorn clothing and gifts with embroidered flowers and create a very personal touch.

I hope I have achieved my aim in producing a book that is easy to use with clear and precise instructions. I would suggest you take a little time to look through the pages and familiarise yourself with the layout before you start work.

The opening chapter gives general information on the 'Materials and Equipment' required for working the designs. The next chapter 'Working Notes' contains handy hints and also includes notes for left-handed embroiderers. 'Finishing and Framing' sets out in detail how to wash and press your finished piece and also contains information on framing and conservation.

'Notes for Embroidered Gardens' prepares you for the subsequent chapters which give descriptions of the Strelitzia and Protea gardens. Included are working notes and lists of flowers and materials required. After completing the Strelitzia garden I redesigned both the embroidered *Agapanthus orientalis* and *Strelitzia reginae*. The new instructions, drawings and embroidered samples appear in the 'Flower Glossary'.

The chapter on the 'Garland of South African flowers' contains complete information for working this project.

'Further Projects' includes the sampler of flowers and some other embroidered pieces made by my friends and students.

'The Flower Glossary' gives specific instructions for the individual flowers, including embroidered samples and drawings reproduced in actual size. The flowers are listed alphabetically by their botanical names. Common names vary in different parts of the world so I have chosen some of the most universally used. Instructions for the butterfly and terracotta pots appear after the flowers.

'The Stitch Glossary' gives instructions with illustrations for all the stitches needed to work the flowers in this book.

Appendix A lists for your reference, in numerical order, all DMC stranded cottons with colour names used in this book. Finally, Appendix B contains some notes by Ross Henty: 'The Framing of Needlework'.

The index will help you find a particular flower or stitch. Flowers are cross referenced using both their botanical and common names.

I hope you enjoy this book and derive as much pleasure from working the designs as I have.

Find a comfortable and well-lit place to work with everything you need within easy reach. I like to listen to some beautiful music whilst I work. If you are new to my embroidery start with one of the less complicated flowers such as *Lobelia, Felicia* or *Lampranthus*. Happy stitching!

Diana Lampe, 1997

The Protea Garden with flowers

Chapter 1

MATERIALS AND EQUIPMENT

NEEDLES

For ease of stitching it is important to use a good quality needle.

Choose a needle that takes the thread easily. The needle has to make a hole in the fabric for the thread to pass through. Whilst a small needle will help to keep your work fine, if the needle is too small for the thread you will find it hard to pull the thread through the fabric.

Embroidery crewel needles are used for most embroidery stitches, as the sharp point and large eye make them easy to work with.

However, a straw or millinery needle should always be used when working bullion stitch and lazy daisy bullion stitch. The long shaft and small eye of the straw needle pass through the wraps easily, resulting in an even bullion stitch.

To avoid confusion, I have noted the appropriate needle to use for each flower in the Flower Glossary. To summarise, use:

- ❧ No 7 crewel or straw needle for three to four strands of thread.
- ❧ No 8 or 9 crewel or straw needle for two strands of thread.
- ❧ No 9 or 10 crewel or straw needle for one strand of thread.

NEEDLE THREADERS

Use a needle threader if you have trouble threading your needle. Cut the thread at a slight angle for easier threading. There is a knack to threading your needle and it definitely becomes easier with practise.

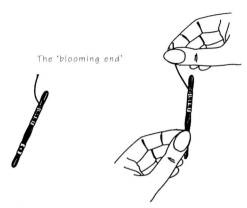

The 'blooming end'

Pulling the threads from the skein

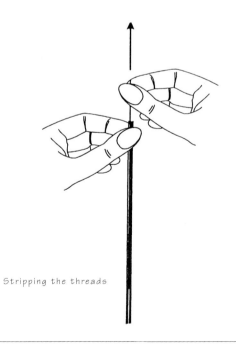

Stripping the threads

THREADS

DMC stranded cotton (embroidery floss) has been used for the designs in this book. It is a mercerised six-stranded cotton thread with a silken finish. It can be separated into the required number of strands. Different coloured threads can be threaded in the needle together to achieve subtle effects and colours. It is readily available and comes in a wide range of colours.

USE OF THREADS

The correct end of the thread to pull from the skein should be obvious. Note also the illustration on the paper band. Do not cut your thread too long. The best length to use is 40cm to 45cm (16" to 18"). This is about the distance from your fingertips to your elbow.

It is important to strip the thread before embroidering to aerate the strands and ensure smooth coverage when the stitches are worked. This means separating all the individual strands of your cut thread, and then putting back together the number of strands you require. When separating your strands, hold the thread at the top and pull the individual strand upwards to avoid tangling.

All spun threads should be worked with the grain. This is important because the thread will twist and unravel if worked against the grain. Run your fingers down the thread to feel the grain; smooth is with the grain, rough is against it.

To ensure you use the thread in the correct direction, always thread the needle with the 'blooming end'. This is the end you pull from the DMC skein. If you are unsure which is correct, flick or rub the ends and the right one will 'bloom'. If your thread has been resting for awhile the 'blooming end' will have become untwisted and fluffy.

FABRIC

In my experience the best fabric to work with is a good quality embroidery linen. It is firm to work with and will last longer than other fabrics. A linen/cotton blend, silk or unbleached calico can also be used for a pleasing effect. If you choose silk, use a light-weight cotton backing. This will add body and make it easier to work. Wash the fabric prior to use as it may shrink.

SCISSORS

A small pair of good quality embroidery scissors with sharp, pointed blades for snipping your threads.

PENCILS

A soft lead pencil (such as 2B) should be used in preference to any other marker. This is because some marking pencils leave chemical residues in the fabric and can reappear or may rot the fabric in the future. Keep the pencil marks light and they will be easily removed when you wash your finished embroidery. If you wish to change the pencilled outline while you are working, remove by gentle rubbing with an Artgum eraser or fabric eraser.

HOOPS

For good tension I recommend the use of a small embroidery hoop [10cm (4")] for couching, French knot stalks and all stitches of the satin stitch family. When working French knots and colonial knots you will have more control and be able to develop a rhythm if a small hoop is used.

A plastic hoop is smooth and good to use. Traditional wooden hoops are also good to use but should be wrapped with white cotton tape to avoid damaging your work. Do not leave a hoop in your work as it may damage or mark the fabric.

Chapter 2

WORKING NOTES

LEFT-HANDED EMBROIDERERS

There is no reason why you should have any difficulty with embroidery because you are left-handed. Just reverse the instructions for the stitches and study a mirror-image of the diagrams. For your reference my second book *More Embroidered Garden Flowers* features a left-handed stitch glossary.

The following suggestions may prove helpful:

- When working flower petals with buttonhole stitch, you will find it easier to work from right to left: as in *Freesia refracta, Thunbergia alata* and the lower petal of *Diascia integerrima.*
- Work flowers formed with buttonhole circles clockwise: as in *Lampranthus roseus. Thunbergia alata* leaves and *Pelargonium* leaves and are also worked clockwise.
- Flowers with petals around the centre should be worked anti-clockwise: Lazy daisy stitch — *Arctotis.*
  Straight stitch — *Osteospermum, Gerbera and Felecia.*
  Fly stitch — *Nerines.*

CLEAN HANDS

Wash your hands frequently as natural body oils could stain your work. In warm weather use a little talcum powder if your hands sweat.

REMOVING BLOOD STAINS

If you prick your finger and the blood stains your work your own saliva will remove the stain. Wet some discarded threads in your mouth and dab onto the stain.

THREADING YOUR NEEDLE
Cut your thread at an angle and you will find it is much easier to thread the needle.

THREADING SEVERAL NEEDLES
Thread several needles before you start so as not to interrupt your concentration and the flow of your work.

NEVER LEAVE A NEEDLE IN YOUR WORK
Do not leave a needle in your work as moisture could cause it to rust which would leave a stain. Make a habit of always pinning the needle to the side of your embroidery.

KEEPING THREADS AT THE FRONT
Never leave a thread hanging free or pinned at the back of your work. You may stitch through the thread and end up with a terrible tangle.

WEAVING IN ENDS AS YOU WORK
Weave in the thread ends and trim them as you work. It is much better to do this at the time rather than when your embroidery is finished.

DO NOT JUMP ACROSS THE BACK OF YOUR WORK
Take care not to carry threads across the back of your work. This could affect the tension, or a deeply coloured thread may show through when your finished piece is framed. It is better to finish off and start again than to run the risk of spoiling hours of work.

ORTS
Cut ends and left-over pieces of thread can be collected in a container and later used as filling for a pincushion or left outside in the garden for the birds to use when building their nests.

STORING THREADS

Some people sort and store their threads by colour and others by project. Most of my students keep their threads in a floss box. I have mine sorted by flower and every flower has its own small plastic bag. I keep all the flowers in this book stored in a box in alphabetical order. Left-over threads can be pushed back into the bag and used later.

You might also find it helpful to store the cut lengths of thread for a particular flower as a book mark with the flower's instructions.

STORING NEEDLEWORK

It is not a good idea to leave your embroidery in a hoop or folded for any length of time. This may leave a permanent mark. A satisfactory way of storage is to roll the work onto a cardboard cylinder with the embroidery facing inwards. The inside roll from kitchen paper, foil etc. is suitable.

If you need to store needlework for a longer period wrap it in archivally sound tissue paper and place it in a box.

STITCHING A GUIDING LINE

Work a small running stitch with one strand of light green embroidery thread as a guiding line for the base of a garden, outline of an initial, or for a garland. This will form a definite and lasting guide and can be stitched over and left in your work.

TRANSFERRING A DESIGN

Transfer a design by drawing freehand with a soft pencil (2B) or use one of the following methods:

- ❧ Place a photocopy of the design onto a light-box (you can make an improvised light-box by placing a lamp under a glass coffee table or taping the photocopy to a sunlit window). Position the fabric over the photocopy and copy the design using a 2B pencil.
- ❧ Trace the design onto paper. Turn the tracing over and redraw the design with an embroidery transfer pencil. Position the tracing, transferred side down carefully on your fabric and press with a medium hot iron for a few moments to transfer the design.

LIGHTING

It is important to consider your eyes and always work in good light. Working in daylight is best of all but a halogen or fluorescent lamp shining directly on your embroidery is the next best. If the light is good you will be able to work for longer periods and find it less tiring.

RESTING

Make sure you have a break from stitching every half an hour or so, to rest your eyes and neck and shoulder muscles. I have found it helpful to focus my eyes on something in the distance for a few moments to relax the muscles. Have a stretch and walk around before returning to your embroidery.

Chapter 3

FINISHING AND FRAMING

When you have finished stitching all the elements in your embroidered piece, appraise your composition carefully for balance of colour, texture and form. Pin it up on a curtain and view it from a distance. You will probably find you need to add an extra flower here and there.

Look outside at your garden and you will see that it is mostly green. If you would like your embroidery to look more realistic, thread several needles with the different green threads used in the embroidery and add stems and leaves throughout. This will give a layered and realistic effect to your work.

Be sure at this final stage to add your name or initials and the year. This is important because you have created a unique piece of decorative art which will be valued by generations to come. Work your signature with small stitches in either stem or back stitch. For this choose a single strand of one of the lighter coloured threads used in the actual embroidery. Green is my usual choice and I suggest DMC 472 or 3348.

When you are completely happy with the balance of your work and it has been signed and dated, it is time for the final touches!

- Tidy up the threads at the back, trimming back so there are no long tags.
- Carefully hand wash your finished work in warm water with soft soap. (Do not soak as some threads may bleed.) Any stubborn pencil marks can be removed with a toothbrush.
- Rinse in distilled water. This will ensure that your heirloom embroidery will not discolour over the years. (Distilled water does not contain the acids and minerals found in tap water that cause brown stains in future years.) Do not wring out the embroidery because the creases can be very difficult to remove.

❧ It is best to iron your embroidery as soon as it is washed. Place a towel on the ironing board and overlay with a pressing cloth. Place the wet embroidery face down on the towels. You can either place another cloth over the embroidery, or iron it direct, but please take care not to scorch it. While ironing, make sure you press any thread tags back over the embroidered part, so that they don't show through the linen when the work is framed.

Now for the exciting bit! When you turn the embroidery over you will be thrilled to see your garden come to life, each flower and leaf looking ready to be picked.

Examine it in daylight to ensure the finished piece is to your satisfaction in every detail. Sometimes a stubborn pencil mark will show and the embroidery will need to be washed a second time.

Keep your embroidery flat and protected in a folder until you take it to the framer. Arrange for framing as soon as possible after washing and ironing.

The final decision you need to make will concern the type and colour of the mount and frame. Choose a mount that complements your embroidery. In my embroideries, I have chosen colours which reflect the feeling of the flowers and of the composition. A good framer will help you make your choice. It is important to conserve your finished piece of needlework, so for further advice on lacing and framing please read Appendix B.

When you bring your framed embroidery home take care to hang it in a place where it will be protected from both natural light and moisture. Do not hang it near a window as natural light will fade the embroidery. It also should not be hung on an outside wall because of the risk of condensation which will cause deterioration.

Chapter 4

NOTES FOR EMBROIDERED GARDENS

The size you wish your finished embroidered garden to be is very much up to you. If it is to be larger than mine, it is important you use a piece of linen large enough to ensure there is ample fabric around your finished embroidery for framing.

You may choose to rearrange the flowers in your garden; perhaps to include some of the other flowers from the book. You could add an ornamental feature or plant from your garden, or include your own pet, a bird or an insect. I am sure you will enjoy the challenge of developing your own original design. As you work keep in mind that your composition will need to have contrasts of colour, texture and form. It also needs to be balanced. One way of ensuring a balanced composition is to look at the work from a distance. This can be done by pinning your work to a curtain and stepping back. The balance can be enhanced by adding an extra flower here and a leaf there.

The following detailed instructions on the order in which to work your embroidered garden may assist you in your design.

Read through the chapter on your chosen project, look carefully at the illustrations, turn to the Flower Glossary and start stitching. Let your garden grow as mine does — freely from the needle and thread.

Included in the following garden chapters is a list of flowers and other inclusions, as well as requirements for each project.

Chapter 5

THE STRELITZIA GARDEN

I designed and stitched most of the Strelitzia Garden prior to my trip to South Africa. The *Clivia miniata* and the butterfly were researched whilst in South Africa and added to the garden when I returned home. The oranges and blues of this garden make a very pleasing contrast and remind me of warm sunny days and clear blue skies which are synonymous with Australia and South Africa. Not only are the colours bright and cheerful but the flowers themselves stand upright, appearing to reach for the sky.

There are several other flowers in the Flower Glossary which could be added to this garden. They include *Anchusa capensis, Crocosmia X crocosmiiflora, Euryops pectinatus, Gazania* hybrid(orange), *Leonotis leonurus* and *Watsonia pyramidata ardernnei.*

Read the chapter Notes for Embroidered Gardens before you start.

Fold your piece of linen up one third from the lower edge. My garden is 27cm (10 3/4") wide (just over the width of this book); centre this measurement on the crease line and mark with a pencil. This will ensure you have ample fabric around your finished embroidery for framing. Work a running stitch along this line with one strand of a pale green embroidery thread. This will form a more definite and lasting guide and can be stitched over and left in your work.

Start in the centre of the garden with the *Strelitzia reginae,* then on the left-hand side of this add the *Zantedeschia elliottiana.* Tuck some *Lobelia erinus* in between. Beside the lilies work the *Gazania splendens* and further along the *Kniphofia praecox.* Add some more *Lobelia* in front to one side and the *Osteospermum fruticosum* at the end. Fill in behind the lilies with the *Plumbago auriculata.*

On the right-hand side of the *Strelitzia* work a group of *Osteospermum fruticosum*. The *Agapanthus orientalis* is positioned next to the daisies with the *Clivia miniata* a little further along. Add three or four more *Gazanias* between and in front of the *Clivias*. Finally at the end of the garden work the *Felicia amelloides*. The butterfly *Danaus chrysippus* is the final touch to your garden.

When you are happy with the balance of the composition, complete your garden by embroidering your signature and the date in stem stitch or back stitch, with one strand of embroidery thread.

FLOWERS AND FEATURES IN THE STRELITZIA GARDEN

Agapanthus orientalis	AFRICAN LILY or LILY OF THE NILE
Clivia miniata	FIRE LILY or BUSH LILY
Felicia amelloides	BLUE MARGUERITE
Gazania splendens	YELLOW GAZANIA
Kniphofia praecox	RED-HOT POKER or TORCH LILY
Lobelia erinus	
Osteospermum fruticosum	SAILOR-BOY DAISY or FREEWAY DAISY
Plumbago auticulata	LEADWORT
Strelitzia reginae	BIRD OF PARADISE
Zantedeschia elliottiana	GOLDEN CALLA LILY or ARUM LILY
Danaus chysippus	AFRICAN MONARCH

PREREQUISITES FOR THE STRELITZIA GARDEN

DMC STRANDED COTTON

blanc neige

ecru

333	blue violet — very dark
340	blue violet — medium
341	blue violet — light
444	lemon — dark
452	shell grey — medium
471	avocado green — very light
522	fern green
721	orange spice — medium
722	orange spice — light
725	topaz
726	topaz — light
739	tan — ultra very light
741	tangerine — medium
791	cornflower blue — very dark
972	canary — deep
973	canary — bright
977	golden brown — light
3031	mocha brown — very dark
3051	green grey — dark
3052	green grey — medium
3345	hunter green — dark
3346	hunter green
3347	yellow green — medium
3363	pine green — medium
3371	black brown
3721	shell pink — dark
3746	blue violet — dark
3772	nutmeg — light

FABRIC
45cm X 30cm (18" x 12")
embroidery linen

NEEDLES
Embroidery crewel Nos 7, 8 and 9
Straw or millinery Nos 8 and 9

Small embroidery hoop 10cm (4")
Soft pencil (2B)
Small embroidery scissors

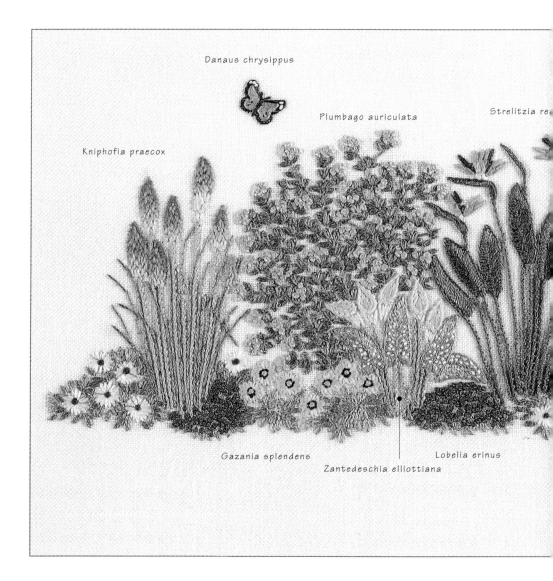

Danaus chrysippus

Plumbago auriculata

Strelitzia re

Kniphofia praecox

Gazania splendens

Zantedeschia elliottiana

Lobelia erinus

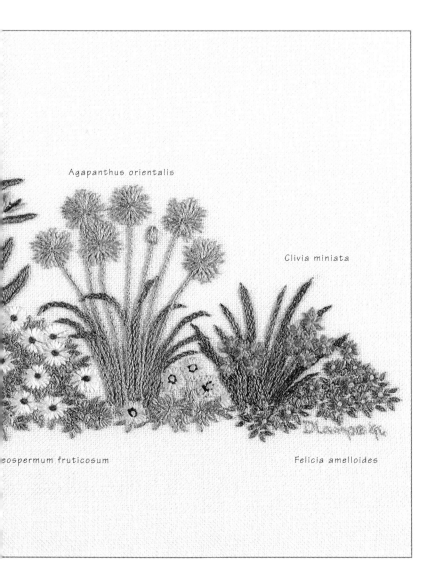

Agapanthus orientalis

Clivia miniata

eospermum fruticosum

Felicia amelloides

Chapter 6

THE PROTEA GARDEN

The *Protea nerifolia X Protea susannae* was the first of the South African embroidered flowers which I designed. This garden literally 'grew' around the Protea tree during a series of classes. New flowers were added as I researched and designed them. My students greatly influenced the developing design. My original plan was for this garden to contain both pink and orange flowers. However I think the resulting garden of different pinks creates a harmonious composition.

There are a couple of other flowers in the Flower Glossary which could be added to this garden; they are *Dierama pulcherrimum* and *Watsonia pyramidata*.

Read the chapter Notes for Embroidered Gardens before you start.

Fold your piece of linen up one third from the lower edge. My garden is 29cm (11 1/2") wide; centre this measurement on the crease line and mark with a pencil. This will ensure you have ample fabric around your finished embroidery for framing. Work a running stitch along this line with one strand of a pale green embroidery thread. This will form a more definite and lasting guide and can be stitched over and left in your work.

Draw or copy the outline of the *Protea nerifolia X Protea susannae* tree onto your linen just to the right of the centre. Work the trunk and branches and start adding flowers and leaves. As there is a lot of embroidering to do to complete the tree I suggest you work on other parts of the garden at the same time. Add the *Osteospermum jucundum* on the left of the tree with the *Eucomis comosa* beside it; and then the *Amaryllis belladonna* with the *Arctotis hybrida* in front. Work the *Gerbera jamesoni* and the *Dietes grandiflora* further along the garden and at the very end place the *Diascia integerrima*. Add the *Rhodohypoxis baurii* along the front of the other plants and the *Coleonema pulchrum* behind.

Leave a small space on the other side of the tree and work the *Zantedeschia aethiopica*. Add the *Gazania* hybrid (cream) and the *Pelargonium cucullatum* on either side. The *Protoasparagus densiflorus* is tucked in behind. Further along are the *Nerine bowdenii* with *Lampranthus roseus* at the end. There are a couple more *Gazanias* in front of the *Nerines* and a single *Gerbera* and an *Amaryllis* behind.

When you are happy with the balance of the composition, complete your garden by embroidering your signature and the date in stem stitch or back stitch, with one strand of embroidery thread.

PLANTS IN THE PROTEA GARDEN

Amaryllis belladonna	BELLADONNA LILY or NAKED LADY
Arctotis hybrida	AURORA DAISY
Coleonema pulchrum	DIOSMA or CONFETTI BUSH
Diascia integerrima	TWINSPUR or PENSIES
Dietes grandiflora	WILD IRIS or FORTNIGHT LILY
Eucomis comosa	PINEAPPLE LILY
Gazania hybrid (cream)	TREASURE FLOWER
Gerbera jamesoni hybrid	BARBERTON DAISY
Lampranthus roseus	PIGFACE OR VYGIE
Nerine bowdenii	GUERNSEY LILY
Osteospermum jucundum	SAILOR-BOY DAISY or FREEWAY DAISY
Pelargonium cucullatum	WILD GERANIUM or WILD MALVA
Protea nerifolia X susannae	PINK ICE
Protoasparagus densiflorus	ASPARAGUS FERN OR BASKET ASPARAGUS
Rhodohypoxis baurii	ROSE GRASS OR ROSY POSY
Zantedeschia aethiopica	ARUM LILY

PREREQUISITES FOR THE PROTEA GARDEN

DMC STRANDED COTTON

blanc neige

210	lavender — medium
211	lavender — light
223	shell pink — light
224	shell pink — very light
316	antique mauve — medium
320	pistachio green — medium
349	coral — dark
369	pistachio green — very light
444	lemon — dark
471	avocado green — very light
472	avocado green — ultra light
522	fern green
524	fern green — very light
581	moss green
603	cranberry
604	cranberry — light
605	cranberry — very light
646	beaver grey — dark
718	plum
725	topaz
726	topaz — light
741	tangerine — medium
746	off white
778	antique mauve — very light
791	cornflower blue — very dark
818	baby pink
841	beige brown — light
938	coffee brown — ultra dark
972	canary — deep
3021	brown grey — medium
3042	antique violet
3051	green grey — dark
3053	green grey
3328	salmon — dark
3346	hunter green
3347	yellow green — medium
3348	yellow green — light
3363	pine green — medium
3364	pine green
3607	plum — light
3609	plum — ultra light
3689	mauve — light
3733	dusty rose
3772	nutmeg — light

FABRIC
45cm X 30cm (18" x 12") embroidery linen

NEEDLES
Embroidery crewel Nos 7, 8 and 9
Straw or millinery No 8

Small embroidery hoop 10cm (4")
Soft pencil (2B)
Small embroidery scissors

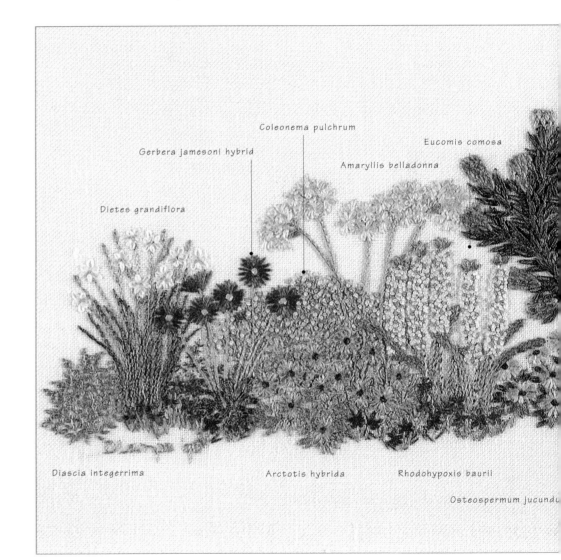

Coleonema pulchrum

Gerbera jamesoni hybrid

Eucomis comosa

Amaryllis belladonna

Dietes grandiflora

Diascia integerrima

Arctotis hybrida

Rhodohypoxis baurii

Osteospermum jucundu

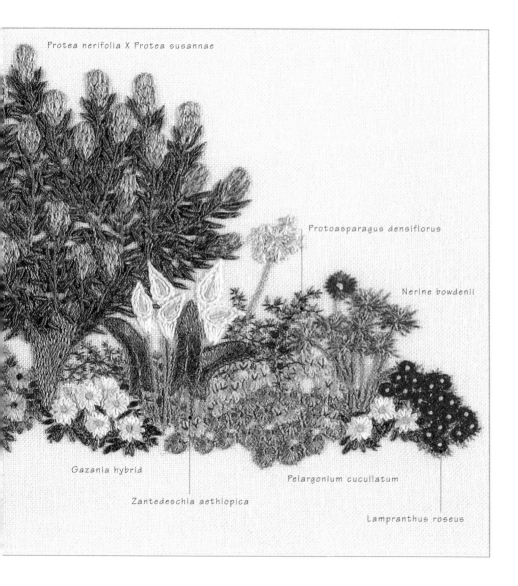

Protea nerifolia X Protea susannae

Protoasparagus densiflorus

Nerine bowdenii

Gazania hybrid

Pelargonium cucullatum

Zantedeschia aethiopica

Lampranthus roseus

Chapter 7

GARLAND OF SOUTH AFRICAN FLOWERS

I find embroidering garlands of flowers to be a very enjoyable pastime. A garland can be quite small if you are only wanting to work on a small project or larger if you are looking for more of a challenge. The width of the garland can be varied and the flowers can be embroidered either close together or with more space between them. The prettiest embroidered garlands I have seen include a lot of greenery. There is probably more work in an embroidered garland than you might imagine so do not fall into the trap of starting with too large an outline. I think that if a garland is too big, it will overshadow the flowers and they will seem to be small and insignificant.

Included in this chapter is a list of flowers, as well as requirements for the garland.

A garland of South African flowers could be worked in a circle instead of an oval if you wish. You may like to add some other or different flowers to your garland from the Flower Glossary. I think the *Anchusa capensis* and *Gazania* hybrid (orange) would be good additions.

As you work keep in mind that your embroidered garland will need to have contrasts of colour, texture and form. It also needs to be balanced. One way of ensuring a balanced composition is to look at the work from a distance. This can be done by pinning your work to a curtain and stepping back. The balance can be enhanced by adding an extra flower here and a leaf there.

Trace the oval lines onto the centre of your piece of linen. To do this use a soft pencil and a light box. Work a small running stitch around both ovals with one strand of light green embroidery thread. This will form a more definite and lasting guide and can be stitched over and left in your work.

Divide the oval into five sections and mark them with your pencil. These sections do not need to be exactly equal in size and are only to be used as a guide. They will help you to embroider a balanced composition without it being too symmetrical.

The following detailed instructions on the order in which to work the flowers in your embroidered garland may assist you with your composition.

Having read through this chapter, look carefully at the illustrations, turn to the Flower Glossary and start stitching.

Begin your embroidery by working the larger flowers and leaves in each of the five sections — *Agapanthus orientalis, Amaryllis belladonna, Strelitzia reginae, Zantedeschia aethiopica* and *Zantedeschia elliottiana*. Add the *Dietes grandiflora, Gerbera jamesoni* (hybrid), *Thunbergia alata, Tulbargia violacea* and *Osteospermum jucundum* amongst the larger flowers and leaves. Fill in with the smaller flowers *Euryops pectinatus, Felicia amelloides* and *Rhodohypoxis baurii*. Finally work the *Protoasparagus densiflorus* emerging from the garland.

When you are happy with the balance of the composition, complete your garland by embroidering your signature and the date in stem stitch or back stitch, with one strand of embroidery thread.

PLANTS IN GARLAND OF SOUTH AFRICAN FLOWERS

Agapanthus orientalis	AFRICAN LILY or LILY OF THE NILE
Amaryllis belladonna	BELLADONNA LILY or NAKED LADY
Dietes grandiflora	WILD IRIS or FORTNIGHT LILY
Euryops pectinatus	RESIN BUSH or YELLOW MARGUERITE
Felicia amelloides	BLUE MARGUERITE
Gerbera jamesoni (hybrid)	BARBERTON DAISY
Osteospermum jucundum	SAILOR-BOY DAISY or FREEWAY DAISY
Protoasparagus densiflorus	ASPARAGUS FERN OR BASKET ASPARAGUS

Rhodohypoxis baurii	ROSE GRASS or ROSY POSY
Strelitzia reginae	BIRD OF PARADISE
Thunbergia alata	BLACK-EYED SUSAN
Tulbargia violacea	SOCIETY GARLIC
Zantedeschia aethiopica	ARUM LILY
Zantedeschia elliottiana	ARUM LILY

PREREQUISITES FOR GARLAND OF SOUTH AFRICAN FLOWERS

THREADS

blanc neige

ecru

210	lavender — medium	791	cornflower blue — very dark
316	antique mauve — medium	841	beige brown — light
340	blue violet — medium	973	canary — bright
341	blue violet — light	3012	khaki green — medium
349	coral — dark	3042	antique violet
444	lemon — dark	3051	green grey — dark
469	avocado green	3052	green grey — medium
471	avocado green — very light	3053	green grey
472	avocado green — ultra light	3328	salmon — dark
523	fern green — light	3346	hunter green
554	violet — light	3347	yellow green — medium
605	cranberry — very light	3363	pine green — medium
718	plum	3364	pine green
725	topaz	3371	black brown
726	topaz — light	3607	plum — light
739	tan — ultra very light	3609	plum — ultra light
741	tangerine — medium	3689	mauve — light
746	off white	3721	shell pink — dark
		3746	blue violet — dark
		3726	antique mauve — dark
		3772	nutmeg — light

FABRIC
45cm X 30cm (18" X 12") embroidery linen

NEEDLES
Embroidery crewel Nos 7, 8 and 9
Straw or millinery No 8

Small embroidery hoop 10cm (4")
Soft pencil (2B)
Small embroidery scissors

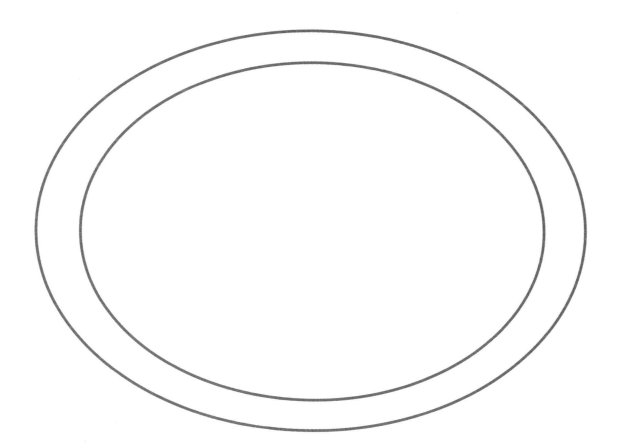

Suggested oval shape and size for embroidered garland

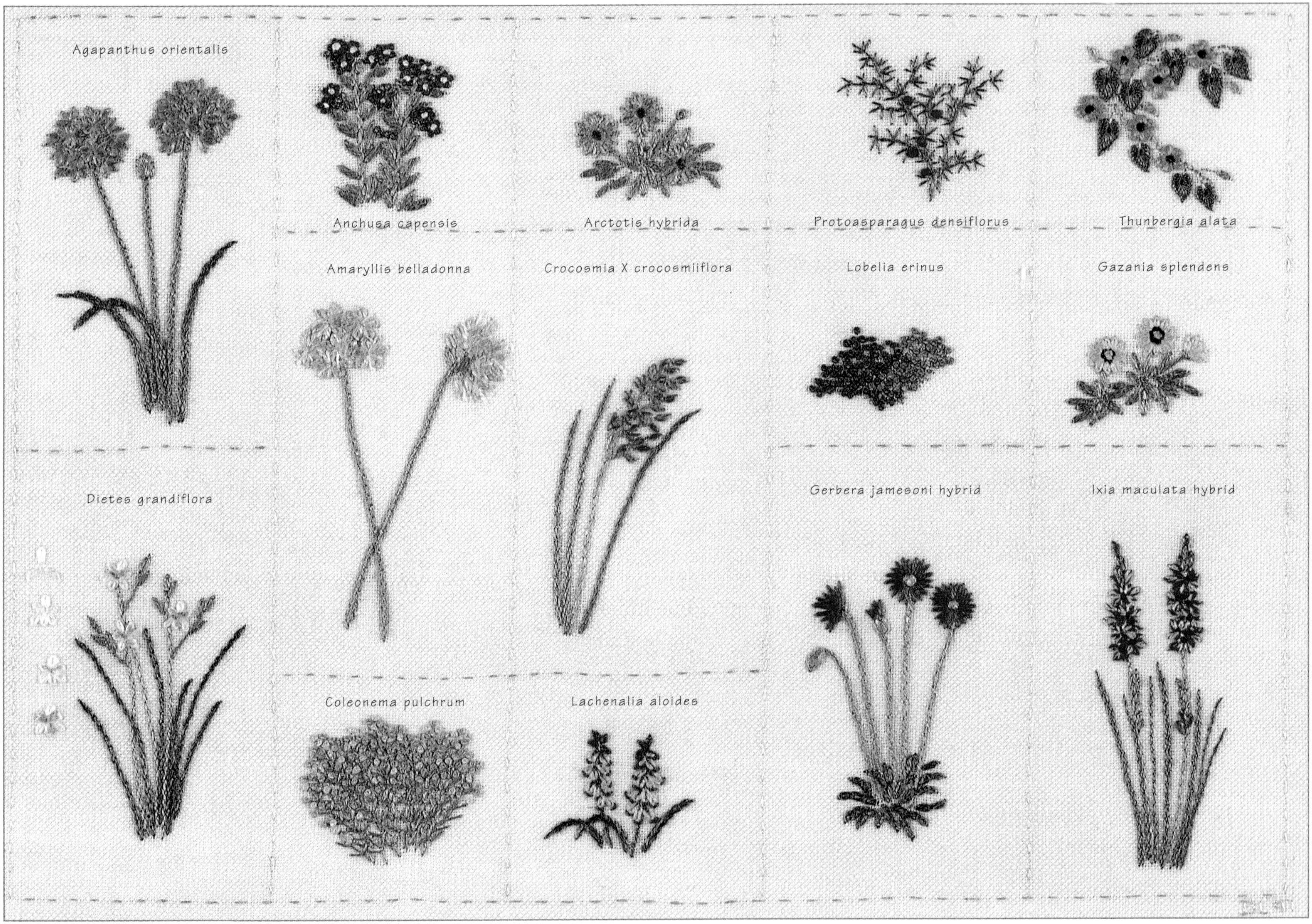

Agapanthus orientalis

Anchusa capensis

Arctotis hybrida

Protoasparagus densiflorus

Thunbergia alata

Amaryllis belladonna

Crocosmia X crocosmiiflora

Lobelia erinus

Gazania splendens

Dietes grandiflora

Gerbera jamesoni hybrid

Ixia maculata hybrid

Coleonema pulchrum

Lachenalia aloides

Chapter 8

FURTHER PROJECTS

SAMPLER OF FLOWERS

All the different embroidered flowers I design are stitched into samplers. They look lovely framed, two or three together with the one matt and frame. Working a sampler is a good way to try different flowers before using them for other projects. Some of my students have made cushions of their samplers.

The grid is reproduced here for you to use as a guide for working a sampler. Trace the grid lines onto the centre of your piece of linen. To do this use a soft pencil and a light box.

Work a small running stitch around the outer border and down the vertical dividing lines with one strand of light green embroidery thread. It is very important for the grid to be 'square' on the linen so stitch along the weft and warp of the linen. Choose the flowers you wish to use and design your sampler around them. Small flowers will need only one section of the grid and taller flowers will need three. Stitch in the horizontal lines as you work the flowers.

When you have completed your sampler be sure to embroider your signature and the date in stem stitch or back stitch, with one strand of embroidery thread.

EMBROIDERED TABLE LINEN

The beautiful table linen was embroidered by Jenny Brennan. She worked
bunches of individual flowers tied with a golden bow in one corner of the
tablemats. The lovely bow is designed by Gary Clarke and is reproduced here for
you. The bow is worked in satin stitch with Madeira Decora thread 1549. The
flowers Jenny has chosen to use are: *Agapanthus orientalis, Amaryllis belladonna,
Protea nerifolia X Protea susannae, Strelitzia reginae, Watsonia pyramidata* and
Zantedeschia aethiopica.

Other embroidered projects made by my students and friends are included on
the following pages of this chapter. These include both an outdoor setting and a
bedroom setting. These will offer you ideas for gift making and some other ways
to use the flowers from this book. Look at them carefully and you will see how
practical and beautiful they are. The silk brooch cushion with the swag of flowers,
the coat hanger and the spectacle case are all particularly lovely and any would
make a very special gift.

Left: Grid for sampler

Tablesetting
Tablemats by Jenny Brennan
China and silverware courtesy Flair, Manuka, ACT
Bow designed by Gary Clarke

Outdoor setting
Garden apron by Bernadette Thomas
Flower carrier by Merrilyn Whittle
Wood carrier by Rita Crawford
Garden gloves by Bernadette Thomas
Secateurs holder by Samantha Kors

Bedroom Setting
Coat hanger by Carolyn Pennington
Brooch cushion by Maggie Taylor
Spectacle case by Madge Guthrie
Hussif by Joan Jackson

Needle case by Joan Jackson
Pincushion by Joan Jackson
Mirror by Bernadette Thomas
Handkerchief by Bernadette Thomas

THE FLOWER GLOSSARY

This glossary gives the colour thread numbers and the method of working for the individual flowers, shrubs, vines, garden ornaments and insects in this book. Also included are the needle type and size you will need to use for each step.

I have used DMC stranded cotton exclusively for the designs in this book. The threads have been carefully matched with the flowers and foliage to create a realistic effect. Many of the flowers come in other colours so you may like to experiment and match some of your own threads. Some colours and subtle effects have been achieved by blending the threads in the needle.

Before commencing work, carefully read the details for each flower, relating the text to the drawing and the embroidered illustration. Remember that the embroidered flowers and drawn illustrations for each flower are reproduced for you in actual size which will help you create the correct sense of scale.

Several flowers (e.g. *Agapanthus, Amaryllis, Clivia, Rhodohypoxis*) have six petals worked from the centre with lazy daisy stitches. Stitch opposite petals first, then fill in each side with more petals.

To depict flowers facing different directions, work the centre of the flower to one side and stitch the petals longer on the near side and shorter on the far side.

Refer to the stitch glossary for the method of working, either to refresh your memory or try a new stitch.

All French knots and French knot stalks in this glossary are worked with only one twist.

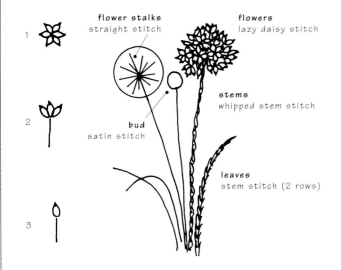

1 flower stalks
straight stitch

flowers
lazy daisy stitch

stems
whipped stem stitch

bud
satin stitch

leaves
stem stitch (2 rows)

2

3

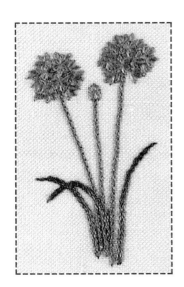

Agapanthus orientalis
AFRICAN LILY or LILY OF THE NILE

THREADS		NEEDLES
340	blue violet — medium	No 8 crewel for 2 strands of thread
341	blue violet — light	No 9 crewel for 1 strand of thread
3347	yellow green — medium	
3346	hunter green	

STRANDS AND STITCHES

flowers	1 strand each 340 and 341 blended, lazy daisy stitch
opening flowers	1 strand each 340 and 341 blended, lazy daisy stitch
flower stalks	1 strand 3347, straight stitch
stems	2 strands 3347, whipped stem stitch
bud	2 strands 3347, satin stitch
leaves	2 strands 3346, stem stitch

Draw circles for the flowers and add the stems and leaves. Work the stems from the 'ground' up into the flower circles and back down with whipped stem stitch. Add a bud with satin stitch at the top of a stem, if desired. Stitch the arched leaves with two rows of stem stitch, tapering to a point for the leaf's tip. Cross some leaves over the stems and over the other leaves for a realistic effect.

Work several straight stitch flower stalks of different lengths radiating from the top of the stems. Fill the flower shapes with clusters of individual flowers, side-view flowers and opening flowers:

1 Stitch individual flowers from the centre with six petals. Work them over the flower stalks.

2 Side-view flowers have two or three petals. Work them at the end of the longer flower stalks.

3 Add opening flowers to the shorter stalks with a single lazy daisy stitch.

Note: *Agapanthus* flowers can also be worked in white.

Amaryllis belladonna
BELLADONNA LILY or NAKED LADY

THREADS		NEEDLES
605	cranberry — very light	No 8 crewel for 2 strands of thread
746	off-white	No 9 crewel for 1 strand of thread
841	beige brown — light	
3053	green grey	
3689	mauve — light	

STRANDS AND STITCHES

stems	2 strands 3053, whipped stem stitch
flower stalks	2 strands 3053, straight stitch
flowers	1 strand each 605 and 3689 blended, lazy daisy stitch
bracts	1 strand each 3053 and 841 blended, lazy daisy stitch
stamens	1 strand 746, French knot stalks

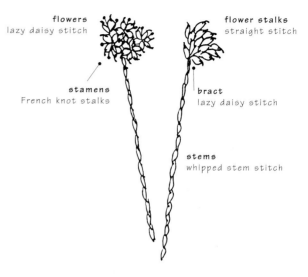

flowers
lazy daisy stitch

flower stalks
straight stitch

stamens
French knot stalks

bract
lazy daisy stitch

stems
whipped stem stitch

Draw the stems which bend elegantly towards the light. Work them up from the 'ground' with stem stitch, add straight stitch flower stalks at the top before whipping back.

Flowers are made up of clusters of five or six individual flowers worked over the stalks. Stitch each of the individual flowers from the centre with six lazy daisy stitches or four for a half-flower. Curve the lazy daisy petals by extending the anchoring stitch around to one side. Add a couple of stamens from the centre of each flower with French knot stalks.

Side-view flowers are worked with a couple of half-flowers and some extra lazy daisy petals. Add the bracts with a couple of lazy daisy stitches at the top of the stem. There are no leaves as these appear after flowering.

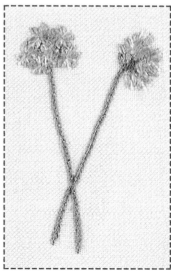

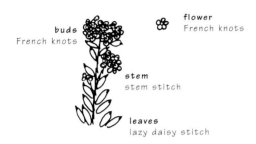

buds
French knots

flower
French knots

stem
stem stitch

leaves
lazy daisy stitch

Anchusa capensis
CAPE FORGET-ME-NOT

Anchusa capensis has true-blue, forget-me-not like flowers and grows to 45cm (18")
tall.

THREADS		NEEDLES
746	off-white	No 8 crewel for 2 strands of thread
792	cornflower blue — dark	
3347	yellow green — medium	
3740	antique violet — dark	

STRANDS AND STITCHES

flower	petals	2 strands each 792, French knots
	centre	2 strands 746, French knot
buds		1 strand each 3347 and 3740 blended, French knots
stems		2 strands 3347, stem stitch
leaves		2 strands 3347, lazy daisy stitch

Lightly mark several branching stems and work them with stem stitch. The leaves
alternate up the stems. Add them with lazy daisy stitches, stretching out the
anchoring stitch at the tip to form an elongated leaf.

Work clusters of two or three flowers and buds at the top of the stems. Each
flower has a French knot centre with five French knot petals. Work the off-white
centre first and surround closely with the blue petals. The petals should be evenly
spaced and touch the centre. To help with petal placement imagine a 'stick
figure' with a head and spread arms and legs. Add some buds with French knots
worked with the blended threads.

Arctotis hybrida
AURORA DAISY

flower
petals: lazy daisy stitch
petal base: French knots
centre: French knot

stems
stem stitch

buds
French knot

leaves
chain stalks

THREADS

316	antique mauve — medium
522	fern green
741	tangerine — medium
778	antique mauve — very light
3021	brown grey — very dark

NEEDLES

No 7 crewel for 3 strands of thread
No 8 crewel for 2 strands of thread
No 9 crewel for 1 strand of thread

STRANDS AND STITCHES

flower	petals	1 strand each 316 and 778 blended, lazy daisy stitch
	petal base	1 strand 741, French knots
	centre	3 strands 3021, French knot
buds		3 strands 522, French knots
stems		2 strands 522, stem stitch
leaves		2 strands 522, chain stalks

Lightly mark flowers with a central dot surrounded by a larger circle. Divide the circle into quarters like a clock face. Work one lazy daisy stitch for each quarter-hour and then fill in between these with two more petals, making 12 petals. Add French knots with 741 at the base of the petals between the lazy daisy stitches. To complete the daisy add in the dark brown centre with a French knot.

Work a few buds with French knots, and the stems for the flowers and buds with stem stitch. Add leaves with chain stalks to fill in around the base of the daisies.

Note: A chain stalk is a lazy daisy stitch worked with an extended anchoring stitch. For the *Arctotis* leaves they are worked in the opposite direction to a lazy daisy stitch. See illustration in stitch glossary.

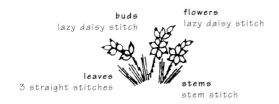

buds
lazy daisy stitch

flowers
lazy daisy stitch

leaves
3 straight stitches

stems
stem stitch

Babiana pulchra
BABOON FLOWER

THREADS		NEEDLES
3347	yellow green — medium	No 8 crewel for 2 strands of thread
3746	blue violet — dark	No 9 crewel for 1 strand of thread

STRANDS AND STITCHES

leaves	1 strand 3347, straight stitch
flowers	2 strands 3746, lazy daisy stitch
stems	2 strands 3347, stem stitch
buds	2 strands 3347, lazy daisy stitch

Work several ribbed grass-like leaves at different angles, each with three straight stitches. Work the centre straight stitch first and add shorter stitches on either side.

Babiana flowers have six petals, work them from the centre with lazy daisy stitches. Position them above the stems and add a couple of side-on flowers with three lazy daisy stitches and an opening flower with one lazy daisy stitch.

Add stems with stem stitch and some buds at the top of the stems with very small lazy daisy stitches.

Clivia miniata
FIRE LILY or BUSH LILY

THREADS

721	orange spice — medium
972	canary — deep
3345	hunter green — dark
3346	hunter green

NEEDLES

No 8 crewel for 2 strands of thread
No 9 crewel for 1 strand of thread

STRANDS AND STITCHES

flowers	2 strands 721, lazy daisy stitch
stamens	1 strand 972, French knot stalks
stems	2 strands 3346, whipped chain stitch
flower stalks	2 strands 3346, straight stitch
leaves	2 strands 3345, stem stitch
	1 strand each 3345 and 3346 blended, stem stitch

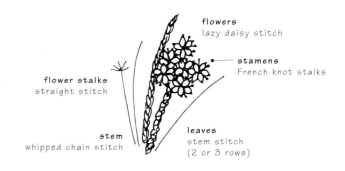

Draw the stems and work them from the 'ground' with chain stitch, add the straight stitch flower stalks at the top before whipping back.

Stitch clusters of flowers over the flower stalks. A flower cluster is made up of five or six individual flowers, each with six lazy daisy stitch petals or four for a half-flower. Add three or four stamens from the centre of each individual flower with French knot stalks.

Add the straight, stiff leaves in both thread combinations with two or three rows of stem stitch tapering to a point for the leaf's tip.

flowers
French knots

foliage
fly stitch

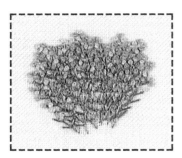

Coleonema pulchrum
DIOSMA or CONFETTI BUSH

This shrub featured in the Protea Garden is the dwarf form and has golden foliage.

The more common, taller growing *Coleonema* is featured in the Winter Garden in *More Embroidered Garden Flowers*. The method of working is similar to the dwarf form, but work a taller bush and use thread numbers 470 for the foliage and 605 for the flowers.

THREADS		NEEDLES
211	lavender — light	No 8 crewel for 2 strands of thread
471	avocado green — very light	No 9 crewel for 1 strand of thread
581	moss green	
818	baby pink	
3609	plum — ultra light	

STRANDS AND STITCHES

foliage	1 strand each 471 and 581 blended, fly stitch
	1 strand of either 471 or 581, fly stitch
flowers	2 strands 3609, French knots
	1 strand each 211 and 818 blended, French knots

Stitch each branch from the top and work in fly stitch down to the base. Overlap some branches and stitch some smaller side branches to create a realistic looking shrub. Work some of the branches with just one strand of either green. Add the flowers with French knots in both thread combinations at the top of the foliage and scattered throughout.

Crocosmia X crocosmiiflora
MONTBRETIA

THREADS

470   avocado green — light

471   avocado green — very light

741   tangerine — medium

946   burnt orange — medium

NEEDLES

No 8 crewel for 2 strands of thread

STRANDS AND STITCHES

stem	2 strands 471, stem stitch
buds	1 strand 741 and 946 blended, lazy daisy stitch
flowers	1 strand 741 and 946 blended, fly and straight stitch
leaves	1 strand 470, stem stitch

Crocosmia tend to grow curving to one side reaching towards the light. Draw the stems which branch out at the top and work them in stem stitch. Add three or four tiny lazy daisy stitch buds at the top of the stems. Now work the flowers with a small fly stitch and a tiny straight stitch in the 'V' of the fly stitch, depicting another petal.

Finally work the grass-like leaves with two rows of stem stitch.

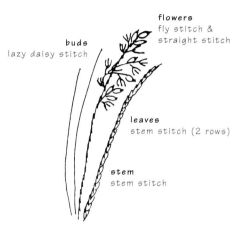

buds
lazy daisy stitch

flowers
fly stitch & straight stitch

leaves
stem stitch (2 rows)

stem
stem stitch

flower
straight stitch
fly stitch

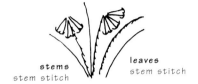

flowers
2 buttonhole stitches

stems
stem stitch

leaves
stem stitch

Cyrtanthus mackenii
IFAFA LILY

There are two different coloured threads given for this flower.

THREADS		NEEDLES
351	coral	No 8 crewel for 2 strands of thread
or		
3823	yellow off-white	
3052	green grey — medium	

STRANDS AND STITCHES

stems	2 strands 3052, stem stitch
flowers	2 strands 351 or 3823, buttonhole stitch
leaves	2 strands 3051, stem stitch

Lightly draw the stems and leaves and work them with stem stitch. Add three or four 'tubular bells' for the flowers at different angles at the top of each stem. Work each 'tubular bell' with two small buttonhole stitches very close together, starting at the left-hand side of the lower edge. 'Kick' the buttonhole stitches out on either side of the lower edge to achieve a bell shape.

Diascia integerrima
TWINSPUR or PENSIES

stems
stem stitch

buds
French knots

leaves
lazy daisy stitch

THREADS		NEEDLES
726	topaz — light	No 9 crewel for 1 strand of thread
3347	yellow green — medium	
3733	dusty rose	

STRANDS AND STITCHES

flowers	1 strand 3733, buttonhole stitch and lazy daisy stitch
centre	1 strand 726, French knot
stems	1 strand 3347, stem stitch
buds	1 strand 3347, French knots
leaves	1 strand 3347, lazy daisy stitch

centre:
French knots

flowers

upper & side petals:
lazy daisy stitch

lower petal:
3 buttonhole stitches

Working from the flower's centre stitch the lower petal with three very small buttonhole stitches, the side petals with two very small lazy daisy stitches and the upper petals with two tiny lazy daisy stitches. Add in the French knot centre.

Work the stems in stem stitch with a few French knot buds at the top and finally add lazy daisy leaves.

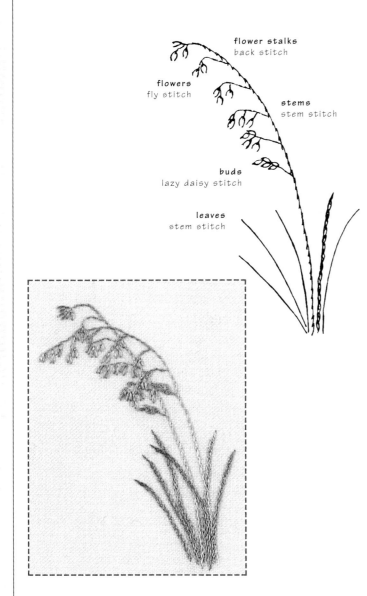

flower stalks
back stitch

flowers
fly stitch

stems
stem stitch

buds
lazy daisy stitch

leaves
stem stitch

Dierama pulcherrimum
WAND FLOWER, FAIRY BELLS, ANGEL'S FISHING ROD
or HAIRBELLS

Graceful *Dierama* grows to 2m (7ft) tall and bends with the weight of it's bell-shaped pendulous flowers. It's beauty has captured the imagination of flower lovers and as a result it has collected many romantic common names.

THREADS		NEEDLES
209	lavender — dark	No 8 crewel for 2 strands of thread
3013	khaki green — light	No 9 crewel for 1 strand of thread
3347	yellow green — medium	
3609	plum — ultra light	

STRANDS AND STITCHES

stems	1 strand 3013, stem stitch
buds	1 strand 3013, lazy daisy stitch
flower stalks	1 strand 3013, back stitch
flowers	1 strand each 209 and 3609 blended, fly stitch
leaves	1 strand 3347, stem stitch

Lightly draw the tall, bending stems and work them with stem stitch and add the arching flower stalks with back stitch.

Add three or four fly stitch flowers hanging from each flower stalk with the blended threads. Add some lazy daisy buds to the flower stalks lower down the stem and also an odd one through the flowers higher up the stem.

Pencil in the grass-like leaves and work them with two rows of stem stitch.

Dietes grandiflora
WILD IRIS or FORTNIGHT LILY

THREADS		NEEDLES
blanc neige		No 8 crewel for 2 strands of thread
210	lavender — medium	No 9 crewel for 1 strand of thread
444	lemon — dark	
3051	green grey — dark	
3346	hunter green	
3347	yellow green — medium	

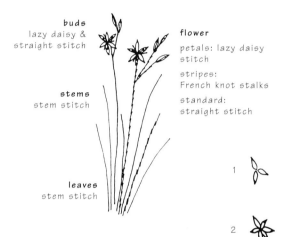

buds
lazy daisy &
straight stitch

flower
petals: lazy daisy
stitch

stripes:
French knot stalks

standard:
straight stitch

stems
stem stitch

leaves
stem stitch

STRANDS AND STITCHES

flower	petals (falls)	2 strands blanc neige, lazy daisy stitch
	stripe	1 strand 444, French knot stalk
	standard	2 strands 210, straight stitch
stems		1 strand 3347, stem stitch
buds		1 strand 3347, lazy daisy stitch and straight stitch
leaves		1 strand each 3346 and 3051 blended, stem stitch

Work the iris flowers first from the centre in the following manner:

1. Leave a small space in the centre and stitch three evenly spaced white petals (falls) with lazy daisy stitch.

2. From the centre stitch three smaller white petals to lie between the first three petals.

3. Add yellow stripes to the three top petals with French knot stalks.

4. To complete the flower add the standard with three mauve straight stitches. Work each stitch down into the centre and slightly offset from the stripes.

    Work the stems with stem stitch and the buds at the top with lazy daisy stitch.

Add a straight stitch into the lazy daisy stitch to fill the bud. Finally work the sword like leaves with stem stitch.

Note: Dietes bicolor is worked as above. Thread colours for the flowers (petals and standard) are 445 and the spots (stripes) in 898.

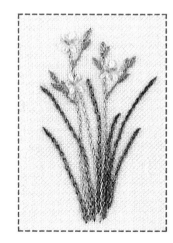

1

2

3

4

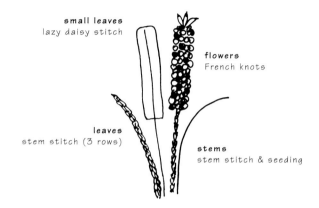

small leaves
lazy daisy stitch

flowers
French knots

leaves
stem stitch (3 rows)

stems
stem stitch & seeding

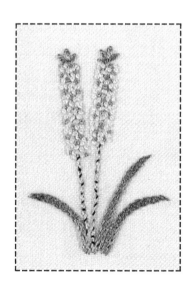

Eucomis comosa
PINEAPPLE LILY

THREADS

369	pistachio green — very light	
471	avocado green — very light	
746	off-white	
938	coffee brown — ultra dark	
3042	antique violet — very light	
3347	yellow green — medium	

NEEDLES

No 8 crewel for 2 strands of thread
No 9 crewel for 1 strand of thread

STRANDS AND STITCHES

stem	2 strands 471, stem stitch
spots	1 strand 938, seeding
small leaves	2 strands 3347, lazy daisy stitch
flower	1 strand each 369 and 746 blended, French knots
centre	2 strands 3042, French knot
large leaves	2 strands 3347, stem stitch

Lightly mark the stems and the rectangular shape for the flower spikes. Work the stems in stem stitch and add the spots to the lower stem with seeding (small back stitches). Changing to the leaf green, stitch three or four lazy daisy stitch leaves at the top of each stem.

Before working the flower spikes study the embroidered sample to see the distribution of French knots. The lavender thread is used to depict the centre of each individual flower and the blended threads the petals. Work the flower spikes with French knots in the two different thread combinations. Stitch them closely together working over the stem to fill the rectangular shape.

Finally work the arching leaves, each with three rows of stem stitch.

Euryops pectinatus
RESIN BUSH or YELLOW MARGUERITE

branches
stem stitch

flowers
lazy daisy stitch
centre: French knot

buds
lazy daisy stitch

leaves
fly stitch

stems
straight stitch

THREADS

523	fern green — light
725	topaz
973	canary — bright
3012	khaki green — medium
3052	green grey — medium

NEEDLES

No 8 crewel for 2 strands of thread
No 9 crewel for 1 strand of thread

STRANDS AND STITCHES

branches		2 strands 3012, stem stitch
flowers	petals	1 strand 973, lazy daisy stitch
	centre	2 strands 725, French knot
buds		2 strands 523, lazy daisy stitch
stems		1 strand 523, straight stitch
leaves		2 strands 3052, fly stitch

Draw the branches and work them in stem stitch, two rows for the major branches and one for the smaller.

Mark a number of small circles with a dot in the centre for the daisies above and around the upper branches. Work the daisies from the centre of the flower, leaving a small space for the centre. Work one lazy daisy stitch for each quarter and fill in between these with two more petals, making 12 petals. Add in the centre with a French knot. Add a few buds between the daisies, each with a tiny lazy daisy stitch. Work straight stitch stems from the daisies and buds back to the branches.

Fill in with fly stitch leaves amongst and below the daisies until a good sized bush is formed. Each leaf is worked with a straight stitch and three or four small fly stitches. Work from the leaf's tip back to the minor branches.

Felicia amelloides
BLUE MARGUERITE

leaves
lazy daisy stitch

petals
straight stitch
centre: French knot

stems
straight stitch

THREADS

444	lemon — dark
3346	hunter green
3746	blue violet — dark
3772	nutmeg — light

NEEDLES
No 8 crewel for 2 strands of thread

STRANDS AND STITCHES

flowers	petals	2 strands 3746, straight stitch
	centre	2 strands 444, French knot
stems		2 strands 3772, straight stitch
leaves		2 strands 3346, lazy daisy stitch

Mark small circles with a dot in the centre for the daisies. Work the daisies with straight stitch petals from the outside edge of the flower, down into the centre. Leave a small space for the centre. Work one stitch for each quarter and fill in between these with two more petals, making 12 petals. Add in the centres with a French knot.

Work stems from the daisies with straight stitches and add small lazy daisy stitch leaves amongst and below the flowers.

Freesia refracta
FREESIAS

Today's *Freesias* come in many different colours, you may like to experiment for yourself. Blending the threads gives an interesting and realistic effect. See Note for mauve Freesias.

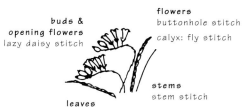

buds &
opening flowers
lazy daisy stitch

flowers
buttonhole stitch
calyx: fly stitch

stems
stem stitch

leaves
stem stitch (2 rows)

THREADS		NEEDLES
742	tangerine — light	No 8 crewel for 2 strands of thread
743	yellow — medium	No 9 crewel for 1 strand of thread
746	off-white	
3347	yellow green — medium	

STRANDS AND STITCHES

stems	1 strand 3347, stem stitch
buds	1 strand 3347, lazy daisy stitch
calyxes	1 strand 3347, fly stich
flowers	2 strands 743, buttonhole stitch
	1 strand each 743 and 742 blended, buttonhole stitch
	1 strand each 743 and 746 blended, buttonhole stitch
opening flowers	thread combinations as for flowers, lazy daisy stitch
leaves	1 strand 3347, stem stitch

Draw stems which bend towards the top for the flowers. Work the stems with stem stitch and add one or two buds at the ends with lazy daisy stitch. Do not finish off the green thread but keep at hand (always on top of your work) so you can add the calyxes after working the flowers.

The flowers are positioned slightly above the stem, using just one thread combination per stem. Working along the stem add one or two opening flowers and three or four flowers. Work each opening flower with a single lazy daisy stitch and each flower with two small buttonhole stitches very close together. Turn your embroidery upside down to work the flowers and start stitching each flower at the left-hand side of the lower edge.

Attach each flower and opening flower to the stem with a tiny fly stitch calyx. Add the grass-like leaves, each with two rows of stem stitch.

Note: Suggested thread colours for mauve *Freesias* are 210, 746 and 3042. Follow the instructions above and work the flowers and opening flowers with the following thread combinations: 2 strands of 210, 1 strand each 210 and 746 blended, and 1 strand each 210 and 3042 blended.

Galtonia candicans
BERG LILY

THREADS
746   off-white
3348   yellow green — light
3363   pine green — medium

NEEDLES
No 8 crewel for 2 strands of thread

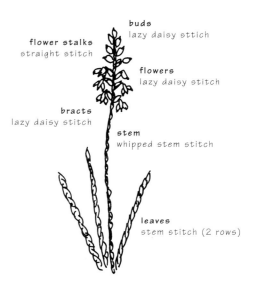

STRANDS AND STITCHES

stems	2 strands 3363, whipped stem stitch
flower stalks	2 strands 3363, straight stitch
buds	2 strands 3348, lazy daisy stitch
bracts	2 strands 3348, lazy daisy stitch
flowers	2 strands 746, lazy daisy stitch
leaves	2 strands 3363, stem stitch

Lightly draw the stems and leaves. Work the stem with whipped stem stitch. Add the flower stalks with straight stitch alternately down the stems.

Stitch several buds at the top of the stem with small lazy daisy stitches. Add the bracts with a small lazy daisy stitch at an upward angle, emerging from below each flower stalk.

Each flower consists of three lazy daisy stitches, attached to a stalk. Work each flower with a long lazy daisy stitch for the middle and two tiny stitches tucked in on either side to form the open bell-like shape.

Finally work the straight, stiff leaves with two rows of stem stitch.

centres
French knots

petals
lazy daisy stitch

stems
straight stitch

leaves
chain stalks
& fly stitch

bud: fly and lazy
daisy stitches

leaf: chain stalk

leaf underside:
straight stitch

leaf: fly stitch

flower

petals: lazy
daisy stitch

petals base:
straight stitch

centre:
French knot

Gazania hybrid (cream)
TREASURE FLOWER

THREADS			NEEDLES
444	lemon — dark		No 7 crewel for 3 strands of thread
524	fern green — very light		No 8 crewel for 2 strands of thread
746	off-white		No 9 crewel for 1 strand of thread
972	canary — deep		
3051	green grey — dark		
3348	yellow green — light		

STRANDS AND STITCHES

flower	petals	2 strands 746, lazy daisy stitch
	petal base	1 strand 444, straight stitch
	centre	3 strands 972, French knot
stems		2 strands 3348, straight stitch
buds		2 strands 3348, fly stitch and lazy daisy stitch
leaves		2 strands 3051, chain stalk and fly stitch
	leaf underside	1 strand 524, straight stitch

Lightly mark the flowers with a tiny circle surrounded by a larger circle. Work the flowers from the centre, leaving a small space for the centre. Work one lazy daisy stitch petal for each quarter and then fill in between these with two more petals, making 12 petals. Add small straight stitches at the base of each lazy daisy stitch petal from the centre into each petal with 444. Finally work the centre with a French knot in 972.

Work a stem from each flower with a straight stitch, couched if necessary and a stem with a bud if desired. The bud is formed with a small lazy daisy stitch inside a fly stitch. Add the leaves with chain stalks and a few with fly stitch forming a clump. Add a straight stitch with one strand of 524 to some of the chain stalk leaves to give just a hint of their lighter underside.

Note: A chain stalk is a lazy daisy stitch worked with an extended anchoring stitch. For *Gazania* leaves they are worked in the opposite direction to a lazy daisy stitch.

Gazania hybrid (orange)
TREASURE FLOWER

THREADS

524	fern green — very light
720	orange spice — dark
730	olive green — very dark
783	topaz — medium
3051	green grey — dark
3348	yellow green — light

NEEDLES

No 7 crewel for 3 strands of thread
No 8 crewel for 2 strands of thread
No 9 crewel for 1 strand of thread

centres
French knots

petals
lazy daisy stitch

stems
straight stitch

leaves
chain stalks
& fly stitch

bud: fly and lazy
daisy stitches

leaf: chain stalk

leaf underside:
straight stitch

leaf: fly stitch

flower

petals: lazy
daisy stitch

petals base:
straight stitch

centre:
French knot

STRANDS AND STITCHES

flower	petals	1 strand each 720 and 783 blended, lazy daisy stitch
	petal base	1 strand 730, straight stitch
	centre	3 strands 783, French knot
buds		2 strands 3348, fly stitch and lazy daisy stitch
stems		2 strands 3348, straight stitch
leaves		2 strands 3051, chain stalk and fly stitch
	leaf underside	1 strand 524, straight stitch

Lightly mark the flowers with a tiny circle surrounded by a larger circle. Work the flowers from the centre, leaving a small space for the centre. Work one lazy daisy stitch for each quarter and then fill in between these with two more petals, making 12 petals. Add small straight stitches at the base of each lazy daisy stitch petal from the centre into each petal with 730. Finally work the centre with a French knot in 783.

Work a stem from each flower with a straight stitch, couched if necessary and a stem with a bud if desired. The bud is formed with a small lazy daisy stitch inside a fly stitch. Add the leaves with chain stalks and a few with fly stitch forming a clump. Add a straight stitch with one strand of 524 to some of the chain stalk leaves to give just a hint of their lighter underside.
Note: A chain stalk is a lazy daisy stitch worked with an extended anchoring stitch. For *Gazania* leaves they are worked in the opposite direction to a lazy daisy stitch.

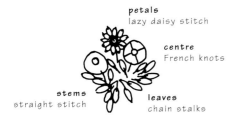

petals
lazy daisy stitch

centre
French knots

stems
straight stitch

leaves
chain stalks

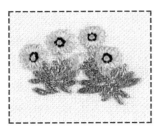

Gazania splendens
YELLOW GAZANIA

THREADS		NEEDLES
522	fern green	No 7 crewel for 3 strands of thread
972	canary — deep	No 8 crewel for 2 strands of thread
973	canary — bright	No 9 crewel for 1 strand of thread
3371	black brown	

STRANDS AND STITCHES

flower	petals	2 strands 973, lazy daisy stitch
	centre	1 strand 3371, French knots
		3 strands 972, French knot
stems		2 strands 522, straight stitch
leaves		2 strands 522, chain stalks

Lightly mark the flowers with a tiny circle surrounded by a larger circle. Work the flowers from the centre leaving a small space for the centre. Work one lazy daisy stitch petal for each quarter and then fill in between these with two more petals, making 12 petals. To work the centre of the flower, firstly stitch French knots around the inside circle with black brown and then add in the centre with a French knot in 972. If desired work a side-view flower with four or five petals and attach it to the stem with a tiny fly stitch calyx (522).

Work a stem from each flower with a straight stitch and add leaves with chain stalks to form a clump.

Note: A chain stalk is a lazy daisy stitch worked with an extended anchoring stitch. For *Gazania* leaves they are worked in the opposite direction to a lazy daisy stitch.

Gerbera jamesoni hybrid
BARBERTON DAISY

Todays popular *Gerbera* hybrids are all derived from the original single scarlet Barberton daisy. They come in a wide range of colours in both single and double forms.

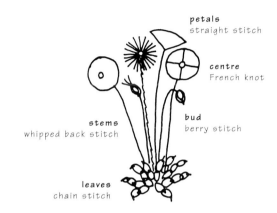

petals
straight stitch

centre
French knot

bud
berry stitch

stems
whipped back stitch

leaves
chain stitch

THREADS		NEEDLES
472	avocado green — ultra light	No 8 crewel for 2 strands of thread
3328	salmon — dark	No 7 crewel for 3 strands of thread
3346	hunter green	
3364	pine green	

STRANDS AND STITCHES

flowers	petals	2 strands 3328, straight stitch
	centre	3 strands 472, French knot
buds		2 strands 3364, double lazy daisy stitch
stems		2 strands 3364, whipped backstitch
leaves		2 strands 3346, chain stitch

Draw stems and circles for flowers with a smaller circle in the middle. Work one straight stitch petal from the outside down into the centre circle (leave space in centre) for each quarter and then fill in between these with about four more straight stitch petals, making approximately 20 petals. Add in the centre with a French knot. Work a flower with a few straight stitches to depict a side view.

Work a stem for each flower with whipped back stitch, adding a small fly stitch calyx to the side-view flower. Work a couple of stems for buds, one of them arching. Stitch buds with a small double lazy daisy stitch (berry stitch) and add a few straight stitches in 3328 to one bud to depict an unfolding flower.

Add the chain stitch leaves at the base of the plant. Each leaf is made up of two or three chain stitches curving slightly to one side.

Note: Other suggested flower colours for *Gerberas* are 353, 349, 3801 and 3823.

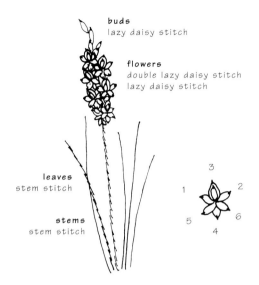

buds
lazy daisy stitch

flowers
double lazy daisy stitch
lazy daisy stitch

leaves
stem stitch

stems
stem stitch

Gladiolus hybrid

GLADIOLI or SWORD LILY

THREADS

471 avocado green — very light
3341 apricot
3347 yellow green — medium
3363 pine green — medium

NEEDLES

No 8 crewel for 2 strands of thread

STRANDS AND STITCHES

flowers	2 strands 3341, lazy daisy and double lazy daisy stitch
stems	2 strands 471, stem stitch
buds	2 strands 471, lazy daisy stitch
leaves	1 strand each 3347 and 3363 blended, stem stitch

Draw the tall stems and work them with stem stitch. Add two or three lazy daisy stitch buds and an opening bud at the top of the stem. The opening bud has a lazy daisy stitch in the apricot thread emerging from the bud.

Each flower spike has several individual flowers alternating down the stem and the individual flowers have six petals. Study the illustration for the placement of the petals and work them as follows:

1. The upper side petals (1 and 2) are stitched first. Work two lazy daisy stitches at a slightly upward angle from the centre (leave a tiny space in the centre).
2. Add the upper petal (3) from the centre with a double lazy daisy stitch.
3. The lower petals are smaller and are all worked from the centre. Stitch in the lower petal (4) with a lazy daisy stitch.
4. Finally work the lower side petals (5 and 6) at a slightly downward angle with lazy daisy stitches. Work petal five first and then petal six to overlap.

Draw the sword-shaped leaves and work them with stem stitch.

There are 105 species from this genus indigenous to South Africa. Modern hybrids with their stately spikes of large flowers have been cultivated from the original species. The Latin generic name *Gladiolus* means 'small sword' and describes the sword-shaped leaves.

Ixia maculata **hybrid**
AFRICAN CORN LILY or WAND FLOWER

THREADS

602   cranberry — medium
745   yellow — light pale
915   plum — dark
3346   hunter green
3347   yellow-green — medium

NEEDLES

No 8 crewel for 2 strands of thread
No 9 crewel for 1 strand of thread

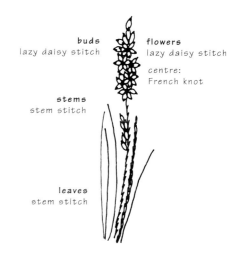

buds
lazy daisy stitch

flowers
lazy daisy stitch

centre:
French knot

stems
stem stitch

leaves
stem stitch

STRANDS AND STITCHES

stems	1 strand 3347, stem stitch
tight buds	1 strand 3347, lazy daisy stitch
buds	1 strand each 602 and 3347 blended, lazy daisy stitch
flowers	1 strand each 745 and 602 blended, lazy daisy stitch
'eye'	2 strands 915, French knot
leaves	1 strand 3346, stem stitch

Draw and work the tall, straight stems with stem stitch. At the top of the stems add a few lazy daisy stitch buds and then some flowers down the stems. The flowers open in the sun to show a dark eye in their centre. Stitch six very small lazy daisy petals for each flower and add in the French knot 'eye'. Add a few extra lazy daisy stitch petals tucked in beside the flowers to depict side-view flowers.

Work a second flower spike with tight buds and buds growing up from lower down the stem. Finally pencil in and work the grass-like leaves with two rows of stem stitch and some with one row of stem stitch.

Note: Ixia viridflora (Blue Ixia) is worked as above, but with taller stems. The thread colours for the flowers are 3816 and 828 blended together, and 791 for the 'eye'.

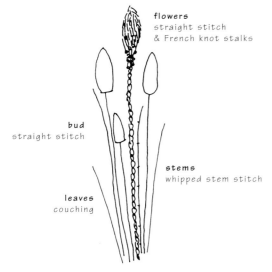

flowers
straight stitch
& French knot stalks

bud
straight stitch

stems
whipped stem stitch

leaves
couching

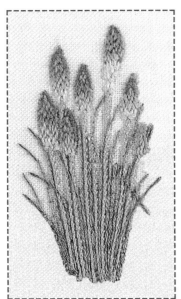

Kniphofia praecox
RED-HOT POKER or TORCH LILY

THREADS		NEEDLES
471	avocado green — very light	No 7 crewel for 3 strands of thread
721	orange spice — medium	No 8 crewel for 2 strands of thread
722	orange spice — light	No 9 crewel for 1 strand of thread
726	topaz — light	
3363	pine green — medium	

STRANDS AND STITCHES

flowers	2 strands 721, straight stitch
	2 strands 722, straight stitch
	2 strands 726, French knot stalks
bud	1 strand each 722 and 471 blended, straight stitch
stems	2 strands 471, whipped stem stitch
leaves	2 strands and one strand 3363, couching

Pencil in the flower shapes and the stems. Work the flowers from the top with small straight stitches graduating from the deeper orange through to medium orange. The straight stitches should not be too even, work some at an angle towards the outer edge of the flower. Add yellow French knot stalks to the lower edge to complete the flower. Vary the shape of the flowers, check the illustration.

Work a bud in straight stitch with the blended threads. Add the stems with whipped stem stitch and the long leaves with couching. Bend one of the leaves over for a realistic touch.

Note: Be sure to use a small hoop for good tension when couching the leaves.

Lachenalia aloides
SOLDIER BOYS or CAPE COWSLIP

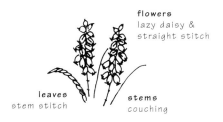

flowers
lazy daisy &
straight stitch

leaves
stem stitch

stems
couching

THREADS
470   avocado — green light
725   topaz
3740   antique violet — dark
3830   terracotta — medium dark

NEEDLES
No 8 crewel for 2 strands of thread

STRANDS AND STITCHES

stems	1 strand each 470 and 3740 blended, couching
flowers	2 strands 725, lazy daisy stitch
and	2 strands 3830, lazy daisy and straight stitch
leaves	1 strand each 470 and 3740 blended, stem stitch

Work the stems in couching with the blended threads. Leave a space between the stems as the flowers take up more room than you might at first think.

Add the bell-like flowers alternately down the stems with small lazy daisy stitches. Start at the top of the stem and work three or four tiny bells at different angles with the terracotta thread. Continuing down the stem, stitch several yellow bells.

Add a touch of terracotta to the yellow bells with tiny straight stitches, one across the lower edge and another into the top. You can also add a yellow highlight with a small straight stitch into a couple of the terracotta bells. Vary these colourings slightly from flower to flower.

Add the strap-like leaves, each with two rows of stem stitch. Work one of the rows of stem stitch a little shorter than the other to form a pointed leaf tip.

Lampranthus roseus
PIGFACE or VYGIE

flowers
buttonhole stitch

centres
French knots

leaves
Straight stitch

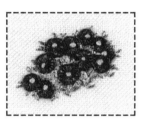

THREADS		NEEDLES
320	pistachio green — medium	No 8 crewel for 2 strands of thread
718	plum	No 9 crewel for 1 strand of thread
726	topaz — light	

STRANDS AND STITCHES

flowers	1 strand 718, buttonhole stitch
centre	2 strands 726, French knot
leaves	2 strands 320, straight stitch

Draw small circles for the flowers and work them with buttonhole stitch. All stitches are worked into the one hole in the centre of the flower. Overlap some flowers to give the effect of a massed carpet of flowers. Add in the French knot centres to the flowers.

Add short straight stitch leaves underneath and between the flowers.

Leonotis leonurus
LION'S EAR or WILD DAGGA

THREADS
611   drab brown — dark
720   orange spice — dark
721   orange spice — medium
3346 hunter green
3347 yellow green — medium

NEEDLES
No 8 crewel for 2 strands of thread
No 8 straw for bullion stitch

flowers
French knot stalks

leaves
bullion stitch

stems & branches
stem stitch

STRANDS AND STITCHES
branches	2 strands 611, stem stitch
stems	2 strands 3347, stem stitch
flowers	1 strand each 720 and 721 blended, French knot stalks
leaves	2 strands 3346, bullion stitch (7 wraps)

Draw the branches and stems and work them with stem stitch, the branches in brown and the stems green.

Add the bullion stitch leaves down the stems and branches, in groups of two or three. Each leaf consists of a bullion stitch with seven wraps. To make the leaf curve slightly extend the anchoring stitch.

Work clusters of flowers with several French knot stalks coming from the leaf nodes on the stems.

Leucospermum cordifolium
PINCUSHION

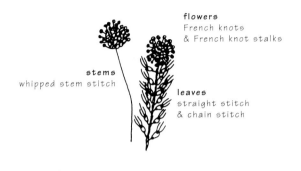

flowers
French knots
& French knot stalks

stems
whipped stem stitch

leaves
straight stitch
& chain stitch

flower shapes

leaf
straight stitch

chain stitch

THREADS

356	terracotta — medium
402	mahogany — very light
471	avocado green — very light
3346	hunter green

NEEDLES

No 8 crewel for 2 strands of thread
No 9 crewel for 1 strand of thread

STRANDS AND STITCHES

stem		2 strands 471, whipped stem stitch
flower	inside (cushion)	2 strands 356, French knots
	styles (pins)	1 strand 402, French knot stalks
leaves		2 strands 3346, straight and chain stitches

Draw the stems and the flower shapes, both inner and outer. Work the stems with whipped stem stitch. Cover the inside flower area (not too densely) with French knots. Add the French knot stalks for the styles or 'pins', work them from between the French knots in an outwards and upwards direction to fill the outer shape. To achieve a full-on flower draw the flower shapes as circles and fill the inside with French knots as before, then work the French knot stalks radiating from the inside to fill the outer circle.

The leaves curve towards the stem. They grow close together and alternate in pairs (decussate). To achieve this effect work the leaves in pairs, on either side of the stem. Add the odd leaf between the pairs stitched over the front of the stem.

Each leaf is made up with a straight stitch with two chain stitches (see illustration). Start at the leaf's tip and work a short straight stitch down towards the stem. Then work a chain stitch around it, followed by a second smaller chain stitch curving back towards the stem and attaching to it with the anchoring stitch.

Lobelia erinus

There are two different blue threads given for this flower. The intensely blue
Lobelia is the most common, but it also comes in lighter blues, white and various
other shades. This is a very rewarding plant to grow in your garden or in a pot.

flowers
French knots

leaves
straight stitch

THREADS		NEEDLES
333	blue violet — very dark	No 8 crewel for 2 strands of thread
340	blue violet — medium	No 9 crewel for 1 strand of thread
3347	yellow green — medium	

flowers
French knots

leaves
lazy daisy stitch

STRANDS AND STITCHES

leaves	2 strands 3347, seeding (small back stitches)
or	1 strand 3347, lazy daisy stitch
flowers	2 strands 333 or 340, French knots

Work the leaves with seeding (small back stitches) or tiny lazy daisy stitches.
Add the flowers with French knots over and above the leaves. Work the flowers
with just 333 or mix the blues to depict a group of several plants growing
together. *Lobelia* is useful for filling in spaces between other plants or for trailing
from pots.

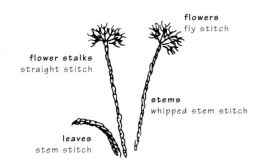

flowers
fly stitch

flower stalks
straight stitch

stems
whipped stem stitch

leaves
stem stitch

Nerine bowdenii
GUERNSEY LILY

THREADS		NEEDLES
603	cranberry	No 8 crewel for 2 strands of thread
604	cranberry — light	No 9 crewel for 1 strand of thread
3347	yellow green — medium	

STRANDS AND STITCHES

stems	2 strands 3347, whipped stem stitch
flower stalks	1 strand 3347, straight stitch
leaves	2 strands 3347, stem stitch
flowers	1 strand each 603 and 604 blended, fly stitch

Draw the stems and work them from the 'ground' with stem stitch, add straight stitch flower stalks at the top before whipping back. Stitch an odd arched leaf with two rows of stem stitch, tapering to a point for the leaf's tip.

Work the flowers with fly stitch. Start with the small 'V' on the outside, passing the long tail over the flower stalks and back to the top of the stem. Work in a clockwise direction and stagger the length of the stitches.

Note: The *Nerine* flowers can also be worked in white.

Osteospermum fruticosum
SAILOR-BOY DAISY or FREEWAY DAISY

THREADS
blanc neige
452   shell grey — medium
791   cornflower blue — very dark
3346   hunter green
or
3363   pine green — medium

NEEDLES
No 7 crewel for 3 strands of thread
No 8 crewel for 2 strands of thread
No 9 crewel for 1 strand of thread

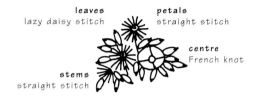

STRANDS AND STITCHES

flowers	petals	2 strands blanc neige, straight stitch
	centre	3 strands 791, French knot
	petal underside	2 strands 452, straight stitch
	odd petals	1 strand 452, straight stitch
stems		2 strands 3363 or 3346, straight stitch
leaves		2 strands 3363 or 3346, lazy daisy stitch

Lightly mark the flowers with an outer circle and a dot for the centre. Do not make them too small. Divide the outer circle into quarters like a clock face. Work one straight stitch from the outside down into the centre (leave space for centre) for each quarter-hour and then fill in between these with three or four more straight stitch petals of uneven length, making 18–20 petals. Add in the centre with a French knot.

The underside of the daisies are tinged with blue. To depict a closing or side-on flower work with a few straight stitches in 452. Add odd petals to the flowers with three or four straight stitches (one strand).

Work a stem from each flower with a straight stitch and add the lazy daisy stitch leaves to form a bush.

Two different green threads have been given for the daisy leaves. Use either green or a blend of both.

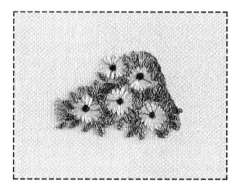

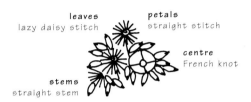

leaves
lazy daisy stitch

petals
straight stitch

centre
French knot

stems
straight stem

Osteospermum jucundum 'African Queen'
SAILOR-BOY DAISY or FREEWAY DAISY

THREADS		NEEDLES
791	cornflower blue — very dark	No 7 crewel for 3 strands of thread
3042	antique violet — light	No 8 crewel for 2 strands of thread
3609	plum — ultra light	No 9 crewel for 1 strand of thread
3346	hunter green	
or		
3363	pine green — medium	

STRANDS AND STITCHES

flowers	petals	2 strands 3609, straight stitch
	centre	3 strands 791, French knot
	petal underside	2 strands 3042, straight stitch
	odd petals	1 strand 3042, straight stitch
stems		2 strands 3363 or 3346, straight stitch
leaves		2 strands 3363 or 3346, lazy daisy stitch

Lightly mark the flowers with an outer circle and a dot for the centre. Do not make them too small. Divide the outer circle into quarters like a clock face. Work one straight stitch from the outside down into the centre (leave space for centre) for each quarter-hour and then fill in between these with three or four more straight stitch petals of uneven length, making 18–20 petals. Add in the centre with a French knot.

The underside of the daisies are tinged with blue. To depict a closing or side-on flower work with a few straight stitches in 3042. Add odd petals to the flowers with three or four straight stitches (one strand).

Work a stem from each flower with a straight stitch and add the lazy daisy stitch leaves to form a bush.

Two different green threads have been given for the daisy leaves. Use either green or a blend of both.

Pelargonium cucullatum
WILD GERANIUM or WILD MALVA

There are over 250 species of *Pelargoniums* indigenous to South Africa. *Pelargonium cucullatum* is an important parent plant of modern garden hybrids.

THREADS
718   plum
3347   yellow green — medium
3609   plum — ultra light

NEEDLES
No 8 crewel for 2 strands of thread
No 9 crewel for 1 strand of thread

STRANDS AND STITCHES
leaves   2 strands 3347, buttonhole stitch and straight stitch
flowers   2 strands 3609, lazy daisy stitch
  stripes   1 strand 718, straight stitch
stems   2 strands 3347, straight stitch

Draw the leaves and work in buttonhole stitch. Add three short straight stitches over the outside edge of each leaf to accentuate the leaf's shape. Check the illustration and embroidered sample.

Flowers are made up of clusters of two or three individual flowers. Stitch individual flowes with two upper lazy daisy stitch petals and three lower lazy daisy stitch petals. Add a stripe to the upper petals with a small straight stitch, worked from the centre of the flower.

Work a stem from each flower with a straight stitch. Some flowers are worked over the leaves and will not require a stem.

flowers
lazy daisy stitch
& straight stitch

leaves
buttonhole stitch
& straight stitch

stems
straight stitch

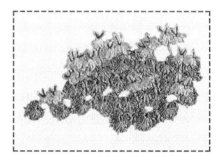

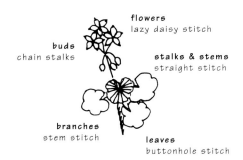

flowers
lazy daisy stitch

buds
chain stalks

stalks & stems
straight stitch

branches
stem stitch

leaves
buttonhole stitch

Pelargonium X hortorum
GERANIUM

Four different colours and thread combinations are given for the flowers of these zonal geraniums: red, coral, peach and pink.

THREADS

red		*peach*	
349	coral — dark	352	coral — light
606	bright orange red	353	peach flesh
coral		*pink*	
350	coral — medium	604	cranberry — light
351	coral	605	cranberry — very light
471	yellow green — light		
3346	hunter green		

NEEDLES
No 8 crewel for 2 strands of thread

STRANDS AND STITCHES

leaves		2 strands 3346, buttonhole stitch
flowers	red	1 strand each 349 and 606 blended, lazy daisy stitch
	coral	1 strand each 350 and 351 blended, lazy daisy stitch
	peach	1 strand each 352 and 353 blended, lazy daisy stitch
	pink	1 strand each 604 and 605 blended, lazy daisy stitch
branches		2 strands 471, stem stitch
stems		2 strands 471, straight stitch
flower stalks		2 strands 471, straight stitch
buds		2 strands 471, chain stalks

Draw the circular and scalloped leaves. Work them with buttonhole stitch, starting at the top left hand side of the leaf, work in an anti-clockwise direction, with all the stitches being worked into the same hole.

Add the flowers above the leaves. They are made up of clusters of three or four individual flowers, each with five small lazy daisy stitch petals.

Work the branches with stem stitch and the stems for the flowers and leaves with straight stitch. Add straight stitch flower stalks, attaching the flowers to the stem. Finally, work a few buds with small chain stalks hanging from the junction of the stem and stalks, below the flowers. Turn your embroidery upside down to work the buds.

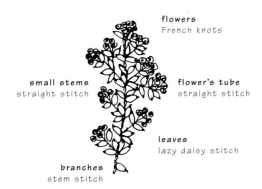

flowers
French knots

small stems
straight stitch

flower's tube
straight stitch

leaves
lazy daisy stitch

branches
stem stitch

Plumbago auriculata
LEADWORT

THREADS		NEEDLES
341	blue violet — light	No 7 crewel for 3 strands of thread
3052	green grey — medium	No 8 crewel for 1 and 2 strands of thread
3346	hunter green	

STRANDS AND STITCHES

branches	2 strands 3052, stem stitch
small stems	2 strands 3052, straight stitch
leaves	2 strands 3346, lazy daisy stitch
	1 strand each 3346 and 3052 blended, lazy daisy stitch
flowers	3 strands 341, French knots
flower's tube	1 strand 341, straight stitch

Pencil in the branches and work them in stem stitch. Add some small stems to the branches with straight stitch. Add leaves in both thread combinations in groups of three or four down the stems and branches.

Add clusters of flowers with several loose French knots just a small distance out from the stem. Add the tubular part of the flowers with a few straight stitches from the French knots back to the stem.

Protea nerifolia X Protea susannae
PINK ICE

THREADS

223   shell pink — light
224   shell pink — very light
646   beaver grey — dark
3051   green grey — dark
3772   nutmeg — light

NEEDLES

No 8 crewel for 2 strands of thread
No 8 straw for lazy daisy bullion stitch

STRANDS AND STITCHES

trunk and branches	2 strands 646, stem stitch
flower stems	2 strands 3772, whipped stem stitch
flowers	1 strand each 223 and 224 blended, lazy daisy stitch
leaves	2 strands 3051, lazy daisy bullion stitch (4 or 5 wraps)

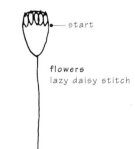

flowers
lazy daisy stitch

leaves
lazy daisy
bullion stitch

stems
whipped stem stitch

start

flowers
lazy daisy stitch

Draw the trunk and branches and work them in rows of stem stitch, several rows for the trunk which then divide into the branches. Add the stems for the flowers with whipped stem stitch coming up from the branches.

Draw the flower shapes and fill them with overlapping rows of lazy daisy stitch in the blended pinks, working from the top of the flower back to the stem. The first row will have five lazy daisy stitches, they sit with their anchoring stitch at the top of the flower. You will need to start stitching this first row a little way down the flower (check illustration). Turn your embroidery upside down and work the lazy daisy stitches back towards yourself.

Stitch the lazy daisy bullion (4 or 5 wraps) leaves alternately up from the stems, curving them towards the flower or stem as you stitch. Cover the tree with leaves, some can be added to the branches.

trunk & branches
stem stitch

Protoasparagus densiflorus
ASPARAGUS FERN or BASKET ASPARAGUS

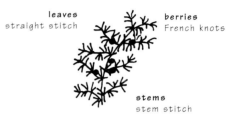

THREADS		NEEDLES
349	coral — dark	No 7 crewel for 3 strands of thread
3346	hunter green	No 9 crewel for 1 strand of thread

STRANDS AND STITCHES

stems	1 strand 3346, stem stitch
leaves	1 strand 3346, straight stitch
berries	3 strands 349, French knots

Draw arching stems with alternating smaller side branches and work with stem stitch. Add groups of straight stitch leaves at intervals along the stem and side branches including the ends. Each group of leaves consists of three or four tiny straight stitches, worked at different angles. Study the illustration for a clear view of their placement.

Add a few red berries with French knots.

Note: Flowers can be added with 2 strands 746 and French knots, if desired.

Rhodohypoxis baurii
ROSE GRASS or ROSY POSY

stems
couching

flowers
lazy daisy stitch

leaves
straight stitch

THREADS

316	antique mauve — medium
718	plum
3363	pine green — medium
3607	plum — light

NEEDLES

No 8 crewel for 2 strands of thread
No 9 crewel for 1 strand of thread

STRANDS AND STITCHES

flowers	1 strand 718, lazy daisy stitch
	1 strand 3607, lazy daisy stitch
stems	1 strand 316, couching
leaves	2 strands 3363, straight stitch

Some of these small flowers are worked with 3607 and some with 718. Stitch them from the centre with six lazy daisy stitches. Add the pink stems with couching and the grass like leaves between with straight stitch. This delightful plant only grows to about 10cm (4") tall.

Sandersonia aurantiaca
CHRISTMAS BELLS or CHINESE LANTERN LILY

This beautiful climbing lily flowers at Christmas time in the Southern
Hemisphere. Please try and find one for your garden, it's graceful form and
lovely golden colour will delight you.

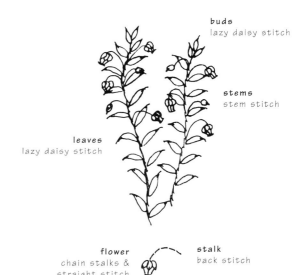

buds
lazy daisy stitch

stems
stem stitch

leaves
lazy daisy stitch

THREADS

470	avocado green — light
471	avocado green — very light
741	tangerine — medium
742	tangerine — light
3346	hunter green

NEEDLES

No 8 crewel for 2 strands of thread
No 9 crewel for 1 strand of thread

STRANDS AND STITCHES

stem	2 strands 470, stem stitch
flower stalks	1 strand 470, back stitch
leaves	1 strand each 470 and 3346 blended, lazy daisy stitch
buds	2 strands 471, lazy daisy
flowers	1 strand each 741 and 742 blended, chain stalks and straight stitch

flower
chain stalks &
straight stitch

stalk
back stitch

Draw the stems and work with stem stitch. Add the lazy daisy leaves alternately up
the stems with a small leaf for the tip. To make the leaves curve extend each lazy
daisy anchoring stitch downwards. This will complete the tip of the leaf.

Work the small flowers next. Each flower is worked from the top with three
tiny chain stalks pointing down and a straight stitch across the lower edge (see
illustration). There should be two or three flowers per stem and an occasional
lazy daisy bud. Add the arching stalks with back stitch for each flower and bud.
The stalks emerge from the stem, above the leaves.

Serruria florida
BLUSHING BRIDE

side-view flower
centre: straight stitch
flowers: lazy daisy stitch

bud
berry stitch

centre
French knots

leaves
straight stitch

branches
stem stitch

flowers
row 1: 5 (open) lazy
daisy stitches

curve anchoring stitch

row 2: 5 overlapping (open)
lazy daisy stitches
centre: French knots

THREADS
223	shell pink — light
371	mustard
470	avocado green — light
472	avocado green — ultra light
778	antique mauve — very light
822	beige grey — light

NEEDLES
No 8 crewel for 2 strands of thread
No 9 crewel for 1 strand of thread

STRANDS AND STITCHES

branches		2 strands 371, stem stitch
stems		2 strands 472, stem stitch
buds		2 strands 472, berry stitch (small double lazy daisy stitch)
flowers	petals	1 strand each 778 and 822 blended, lazy daisy stitch, or 2 strands 822, lazy daisy stitch
	centre	1 strand each 223 and 778 blended, French knots or straight stitch
leaves		1 strand 470, straight stitch

Draw the branches and stems and work them with stem stitch. Add some buds to some of the stems with berry stitch.

Position and work the flowers and some side-view flowers over the bush. Work the flowers from the centre, leaving a small space for the centre. Work the petals with five small, open lazy daisy stitches and then add five more petals to overlap, between them. Extend and curve the anchoring stitches to one side as you work the lazy daisy stitch petals. To complete the flower add the centre with three or four French knots.

Work the side-view flowers with several overlapping lazy daisy stitches. Turn your work and stitch towards the top of the flower. Stitch some of flowers to be less open and some of them to be more open. Add the centres with tiny straight stitches peeping out from the top of the flower. Some of the side-view flowers could be worked with two strands of 822.

Add the alternating feathery leaves to the stems. Work the leaves with three or four straight stitches of different lengths and at different angles.

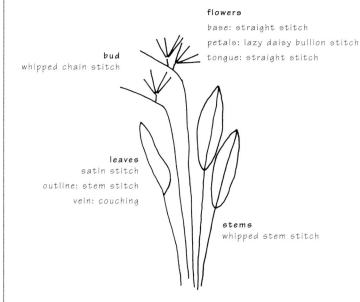

flowers
base: straight stitch
petals: lazy daisy bullion stitch
tongue: straight stitch

bud
whipped chain stitch

leaves
satin stitch
outline: stem stitch
vein: couching

stems
whipped stem stitch

Strelitzia reginae
BIRD OF PARADISE

The *Strelitzia* is a complex flower to embroider. Study the instructions and the illustrations carefully before you begin.

THREADS		NEEDLES
739	tan — ultra very light	No 8 crewel for 2 strands of thread
741	tangerine — light	No 9 crewel for 1 strand of thread
791	cornflower blue — very dark	No 8 straw for lazy daisy bullion stitch
3051	green grey — dark	
3721	shell pink — dark (red)	

STRANDS AND STITCHES

stems		2 strands 3051, whipped stem stitch
flower	bud	2 strands 3051, whipped chain stitch
	highlight	1 strand 3721, straight and stem stitch
	flower base	1 strand 739, straight stitch
	petals	2 strands 741, lazy daisy bullion stitch (3 wraps)
	tongue	2 strands 791, straight stitch
leaves		2 strands 3051, satin stitch or satin leaf stitch
	outline	1 strand 3051, stem stitch
	vein	1 strand 3721, couching

Draw the flower stems extending them into the bud.

1. Work stem stitch from the 'ground', up the stems; stopping just before the stem bends into the bud. Continue with the same needle and thread and stitch the bud with chain stitch. Take your needle through to the back of your work and make a good point for the bud.
2. Bring your needle to the top of your work and whip back to the ground.

3. To the bud, add a red highlight with a few straight stitches angled over the bend and some stem stitches along the top. Finish at the end of the bud with a good point.

The *Strelitzia* flowers vary in composition; some have one flower and some have a second emerging flower. The following instructions relate to just one flower. Work a second flower in the same way next to the first if required. (See embroidered illustration No. 7 overleaf.)

4. Work the flower base from the bud with four short straight stitches.

Each flower consists of three orange petals and a blue tongue.

5. Work the petals with lazy daisy bullion stitch (3 wraps) from the flower base. Stretch them out to form a good point. Point one petal towards the tip of the bud and the other two side by side at an angle, leaning back towards the bend of the bud.

6. Work the tongue between the petals with a long straight stitch and two smaller straight stitches. The tongue opens to the back of the bud.

Draw the facing leaves with central veins and two or three side-on leaves. Add stems to the leaves.

8. Satin stitch the facing leaves with very slanting stitches. Begin at the base of the leaf and work along the side straightening the stitches towards the tip to form a point. Work back down the other side. Alternatively work the leaves with satin leaf stitch (see Stitch Glossary). Outline the leaves with stem stitch and add the red veins with couching. Finally add the stems of the leaves with whipped stem stitch.

9. Work side-on leaves with slanting satin stitch. Add the stem and spine for each leaf with whipped stem stitch. Stem stitch from the 'ground' up the back of the leaf to the tip and whip back down. Finally outline the leaves with stem stitch.

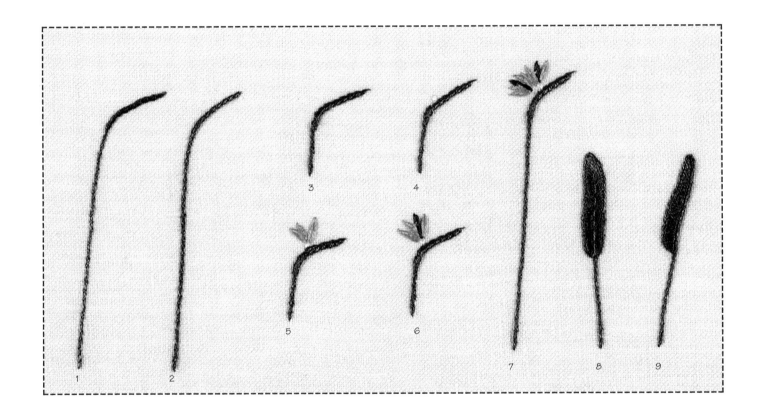

Thunbergia alata
BLACK-EYED SUSAN

THREADS		NEEDLES
469	avocado green	No 7 crewel for 3 strands of thread
471	avocado green — very light	No 8 crewel for 2 strands of thread
741	tangerine — medium	No 9 crewel for 1 strand of thread
3371	black brown	

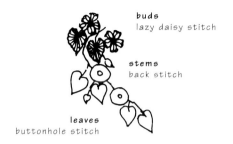

buds
lazy daisy stitch

stems
back stitch

leaves
buttonhole stitch

STRANDS AND STITCHES

vine	1 or 2 strands 471, back stitch
flower and leaf stems	1 strand 471, back stitch
flowers	2 strands 741, buttonhole stitch
'eye'	3 strands 3371, French knot
buds	2 strands 471, lazy daisy stitch
leaves	1 strand 469, buttonhole stitch

flower
buttonhole stitch
eye: French knot

petal
2 buttonhole stitches

start
finish

Draw the twining vine with the heart-shaped leaves. The leaves come from the vine in pairs and the flowers emerge from above them. Draw the flowers with small circles and a dot in the centre. Both flowers and leaves have stems. Work the vine with back stitch, the thicker vine with two strands and the finer with one strand.

Work the leaves with buttonhole stitch, start at the top left-hand side of the leaf and work in an anti-clockwise direction with all the stitches being worked into the same hole. Continue around the leaf to the tip and do an extra little stitch down below it to form a good point, come back up to where you were and buttonhole the other side of the leaf.

Each flower has five petals. When working the petals be sure to leave a small space in the centre of the flower for the 'eye'. Work each petal from the centre

with two buttonhole stitches. Take the thread to the back of your work at the outer edge to complete the petal and secure the buttonhole stitch. Come up in the centre again to start the next petal. Work five petals in this manner for each flower. Add in the black brown 'eyes' with French knots.

Work the flower and leaf stems joining them to the vine with back stitch. Add a couple of buds with small lazy daisy stitch and stems if desired.

Note: Take care not to jump across the back of your work with the black brown thread. Such a deep shade may show through from the back when your finished piece is framed. It may also bleed when washed, so be sure to rinse thoroughly, do not soak or leave sitting around wet. Iron immediately after washing.

Tulbaghia violacea
WILD GARLIC or SOCIETY GARLIC

THREADS

554   violet — light

3363   pine green

3726   antique mauve — dark

NEEDLES

No 8 crewel for 2 strands of thread

No 9 crewel for 1 strand of thread

STRANDS AND STITCHES

stems	1 strand 3363, stem stitch
leaves	2 strands 3363, stem stitch
flowers	2 strands 554, fly stitch
buds	1 strand 3726, lazy daisy stitch and straight stitch

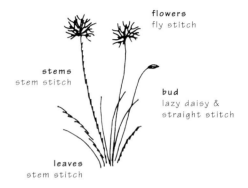

flowers
fly stitch

stems
stem stitch

bud
lazy daisy &
straight stitch

leaves
stem stitch

Lightly mark the stems and leaves and work in stem stitch, one strand for the stems and two for the leaves.

Stitch the flowers from the outer edge in fly stitch with the tails all going into the same hole at the top of the stem. Work in a clockwise direction and stagger the length of the stitches. A couple of buds can be added with a lazy daisy stitch and a straight stitch within. Lace a thread of 3726 through the upper stems of the buds.

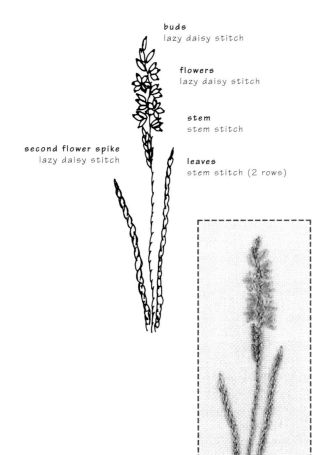

buds
lazy daisy stitch

flowers
lazy daisy stitch

stem
stem stitch

second flower spike
lazy daisy stitch

leaves
stem stitch (2 rows)

Watsonia pyramidata
BUGLE LILY

THREADS		NEEDLES
223	shell pink — light	No 8 crewel for 2 strands of thread
3347	yellow green — medium	
3609	plum — ultra light	

STRANDS AND STITCHES

stems	1 strand each 223 and 3347 blended, stem stitch
tight buds	as for stems
flowers and opening buds	2 strands 3609, lazy daisy stitch
leaves	2 strands 3347, stem stitch

Lightly draw the tall stems (this species grows to 1.7m) and work them with stem stitch. Add a couple of tight buds with small lazy daisy stitches at the top of the stem. Work a couple of opening buds (below the tight buds) with slightly longer lazy daisy stitches.

Each flower spike has several individual flowers alternating down the stem and each individual flower has six petals. Work facing flowers with six small lazy daisy stitch petals and side-on flowers at a slightly upward angle with three lazy daisy stitch petals.

Work an emerging second flower spike with tight buds lower down the stem. Draw the leaves and work them with two rows of stem stitch.

Note: Watsonia pyramidata ardernnei is the white form of the above. Work the flowers with blanc neige and two strands of 3347 for the stems and tight buds. *Watsonia beatricis* is another popular garden species. It grows to 1m (40") high and has salmon or coral flowers. Follow the above instructions, but work shorter stems and leaves. Add the flowers with 1 strand each of 352 and 3326 blended together.

Zantedeschia aethiopica
ARUM LILY

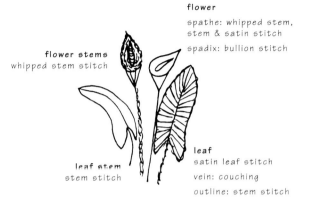

flower
spathe: whipped stem,
stem & satin stitch
spadix: bullion stitch

flower stems
whipped stem stitch

leaf
satin leaf stitch
vein: couching
outline: stem stitch

leaf stem
stem stitch

THREADS		NEEDLES
blanc neige		No 8 crewel for 2 strands of thread
725	topaz	No 9 crewel for 1 strand of thread
746	off-white	No 8 straw for bullion stitch
3346	hunter green	
3347	yellow green — medium	

STRANDS AND STITCHES

flowers	spathe	1 strand each blanc and 746 blended, whipped stem, stem and satin stitches
	spadix	2 strands 725, bullion (7 wraps)
flower stems		2 strands 3347, whipped stem stitch
leaves		2 strands 3346, satin leaf stitch
	outline	1 strand 3346, stem stitch
	vein	1 strand 3346, couching
leaf stems		2 strands 3346, stem stitch

Draw the flowers and stitch around the rim of the spathe with whipped stem stitch. Continue with stem stitch to fill the inside of the spathe, following the contour of the rim. Add a few satin stitches below the rim in a triangular shape to complete the spathe.

To form the spadix work a bullion stitch (7 wraps) inside the rim and towards the point of the spathe. Add the flower stems with whipped stem stitch, work up to the flower, stitch into it and whip back down.

Draw the leaves and check the illustration for stitch direction and work in satin leaf stitch. Add the stems with stem stitch. Outline the leaf with stem stitch and work the central vein with couching.

Zantedeschia elliottiana
GOLDEN CALLA LILY or ARUM LILY

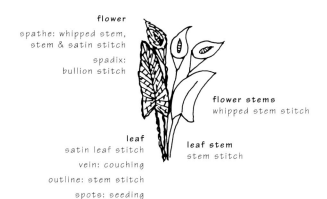

flower
spathe: whipped stem,
stem & satin stitch

spadix:
bullion stitch

flower stems
whipped stem stitch

leaf
satin leaf stitch
vein: couching
outline: stem stitch
spots: seeding

leaf stem
stem stitch

THREADS		NEEDLES
ecru		No 8 crewel for 2 strands of thread
725	topaz	No 9 crewel for 1 strand of thread
726	topaz — light	No 8 straw for bullion stitch
3347	yellow green — medium	

STRANDS AND STITCHES

flowers	spathe	2 strands 726, whipped stem, stem and satin stitches
	spadix	2 strands 725, bullion (5 wraps)
stems		2 strands 3347, whipped stem stitch
leaves		2 strands 3347, satin leaf stitch
	outline	1 strand 3347, stem stitch
	vein	1 strand 3347, couching
	stems	2 strands 3347, stem stitch
	spots	2 strands ecru, seeding (small back stitches)

Draw the flowers and stitch around the rim of the spathe with whipped stem stitch. Continue with stem stitch to fill the inside of the spathe, following the contour of the rim. Add a few satin stitches below the rim in a triangular shape to complete the spathe.

To form the spadix work a bullion stitch (5 wraps) inside the rim of the spathe and towards the point of the spathe. Add the flower stems with whipped stem stitch. Work up to the flower, stitch into it and whip back down.

Draw each leaf shape, check the illustration for stitch direction and work in satin leaf stitch. Add the stems with stem stitch. Add the spots with seeding (small back stitches), outline the leaf with stem stitch and the vein down the centre of the leaf with couching.

Danaus chrysippus
AFRICAN MONARCH

THREADS

blanc neige

977   golden brown — light

3031   mocha brown — very dark

NEEDLES

No 9 crewel for 1 strand of thread

No 9 straw for bullion stitch

STRANDS AND STITCHES

wings	outer	1 strand 3031, buttonhole stitch
	inner	1 strand 977, buttonhole stitch
	white spots	1 strand blanc neige, French knots
	brown spots	1 strand 3031, seeding
body		1 strand 3031, bullion (15 wraps)
feelers		1 strand 3031, French knot stalks

Carefully study the illustration and draw the butterfly with larger front wings and smaller back wings, each with an inner and outer part. Work the outer wings and then the inner wings with buttonhole stitch. Work three white spots on the top of the outer wing. Starting at the head of the butterfly, embroider the body with a bullion stitch (15 wraps), couching in the centre. Add the feelers with French knot stalks and the brown spots on the smaller, inner wings with seeding.

Note: It is difficult to draw the butterfly so I recommend you use an embroidery transfer pencil. Sharpen the pencil and lightly trace the butterfly onto paper. Taking great care, position the tracing, transfer side down on your fabric and press with a hot iron for a few moments to transfer the design.

Caution: transferred lines probably will not wash out of your fabric.

white spots
French knots

feelers
French knot stalks

brown spots
seeding

wings
buttonhole stitch

body
bullion stitch

rim
satin stitch

pot
long & short stitch

outline
stem stitch

TERRACOTTA POT 1

Terracotta pots can be worked in either of the suggested thread colours, or a blend of the two together. It would be a good idea to vary the threads if you plan to have more than one pot in your embroidered design.

THREADS

356   terracotta — medium

or

3778   terracotta — light

NEEDLES

No 9 crewel for 1 strand of thread

No 8 crewel for 2 strands of thread

STRANDS AND STITCHES

pot	2 strands 356 or 3778, long and short stitch
rim	2 strands 356 or 3778, satin stitch
outline	1 strand 356 or 3778, stem stitch

Pencil in your terracotta pot and work in long and short stitch, stitch downwards starting from just below the rim. Work the rim of the pot with a vertical satin stitch. To complete, stem stitch an outline around the pot including the lower edge of the rim.

Note: Use a small hoop for good tension when working long and short stitch.

TERRACOTTA POT 2

THREADS

356   terracotta — medium

or

3778   terracotta — light

NEEDLES

No 8 crewel for 2 strands of thread

No 7 crewel for 3 strands of thread

STRANDS AND STITCHES

pot   2 strands 356 or 3778, long and short stitch, stem stitch

relief   3 strands of 356 or 3778, French knots

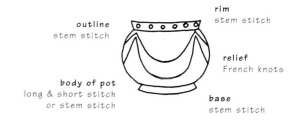

Draw or trace the pot. Outline the rounded body of the pot with stem stitch. Then work the rim with four rows of stem stitch and the base with three. Neaten each end of the rim and the base with a straight stitch. Fill in the body of the pot with a vertical long and short stitch or stem stitch worked across (leave the relief area free of stitches). Add the relief with French knots, including several evenly spaced across the rim.

Note: See *Pelargonium X hortorum* for an example of the terracotta pot with stem stitch filling.

THE STITCH GLOSSARY

Embroidery stitches can have different names and may vary in structure and in the technique of working. This glossary describes how the stitches have been worked for the designs in this book.

For left-handed embroiderers: study the diagrams in mirror-image and reverse the instructions for each step. You may find it helpful to refer to the left-handed stitch glossary in *More Embroidered Garden Flowers*.

STEM OR OUTLINE STITCH

A simple stitch for stems, outlines and filling.

Working from left to right, take small, even, straight or slightly slanting stitches along the design line. Leave a space between the previous stitch and the point where the needle emerges. Keep the thread below or on the same side of your work. For wide stem stitch, make the stitches on a greater angle.

WHIPPED STEM STITCH

Whipped stem stitch gives a corded effect and is useful for stems.

Work a row of stem stitch along the design line and bring the needle to the top of your work. Using the blunt end of the needle and working in the opposite direction to the stem stitch, whip back through each stem stitch, but not into the fabric.

BACK STITCH

Back stitch is useful to form a delicate line and for curves and outlines. It is also a foundation for composite stitches such as pekinese stitch.

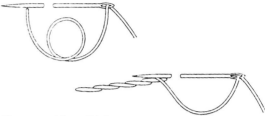

Stem or outline stitch

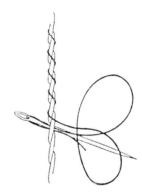

Whipped stem stitch

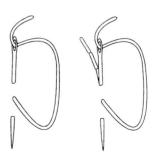

Back stitch

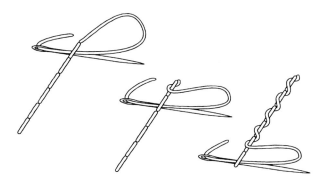

Whipped back stitch

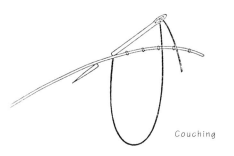

Couching

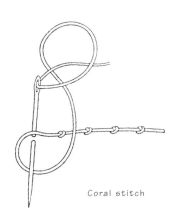

Coral stitch

Take a small, even backward stitch along the design line and bring the needle out the same distance in front. Take another backward stitch and continue in this way along the design line.

WHIPPED BACK STITCH

Work a row of back stitch along the design line and bring the needle to the top of your work. With the blunt end of the needle, whip back through each back stitch but not into the fabric.

COUCHING

The leaves and flower stems in this book worked in couching have two strands of thread laid down and one strand for the tying stitch of matching thread. The use of a small hoop will help with tension. Use two needles and keep them on top of your work to prevent tangling. Anchor the thread not in use and keep it out of the way. Short lengths of couching can be worked with one needle and thread.

Lay the thread along the design line, holding and guiding its direction with your thumb. Tie it down with small straight stitches made across it at regular intervals.

CORAL STITCH

Coral stitch is a simple knotted line stitch useful for flower stems.

Hold the thread to the left along the design line. Take a small stitch towards you with the thread over and around the needle; pull through forming a knot. Continue at regular intervals.

FRENCH KNOTS

When working French knots you will have more control and be able to develop a rhythm if a small (10 cm/4") hoop is used. To increase the size of knots, use more strands of thread rather than more twists.

Bring the thread up at the desired spot. Hold the thread firmly with your left hand. With the needle pointing toward you, place it under the thread from the left-hand side and twist it around once. Insert the needle close to where the thread first emerged, but not in the same hole. Draw the thread around the needle to firm the knot and pull through to the back. Pass on to the position for the next knot.

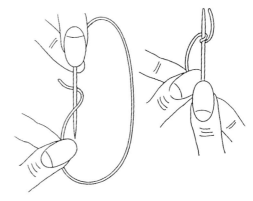

French knots

FRENCH KNOT STALKS

French knot stalks are worked in the same manner as French knots. The use of a small embroidery hoop will help you achieve good tension.

To form the stalk, after encircling the needle with the thread, insert the needle the desired distance away from where it first emerged. Pull through to the back and pass on to the position for the next stitch.

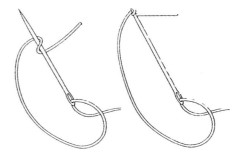

French knot stalks

COLONIAL KNOTS OR CANDLEWICKING KNOTS

This stitch differs from a French knot in that the twists are worked in a figure of eight. It stands up high on the fabric and needs to be worked very firmly. When working colonial knots you will have more control and be able to develop a rhythm if a small (10cm/4") hoop is used.

Bring the thread up at the desired spot. Hold the thread firmly with your left hand. With the needle pointing away from you, place it under the thread from the left-hand side and twist it in an anticlockwise direction away from you. The needle will now be facing you. The second part of the stitch is the same as a French knot. Now place the needle under the thread from the left-hand side and twist it around once back to the original position.

Insert the needle close to where the thread first emerged, but not in the same hole. Draw the thread around the shaft of the needle to firm the knot and pull through to the back. Pass on to the position for the next knot.

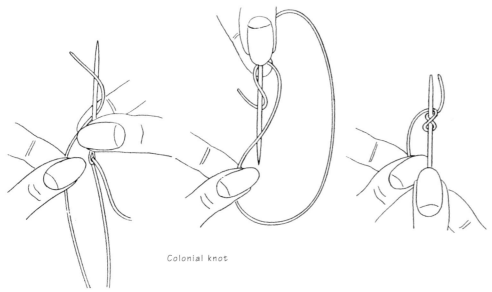

Colonial knot

BULLION STITCH

This stitch should be worked with a straw or millinery needle. The small eye will allow the needle to pass easily through the wraps. The number of wraps should equal the length of the 'back stitch'.

Commence as though to make a back stitch the required length for the bullion stitch. Bring the needle up at the starting point but do not pull through. Wrap the thread around the needle, in a clockwise direction, the required number of times. Do not wrap too tightly. Place your left thumb over the wraps, then pull the needle through the wraps. As you pull the thread up firmly, the bullion will turn back. Adjust the wraps if necessary. Insert the needle at the starting point and pull through to complete the bullion stitch.

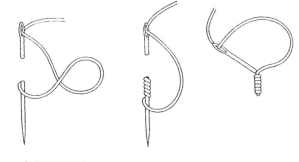

Bullion stitch

LAZY DAISY BULLION STITCH

This stitch is a combination of lazy daisy and bullion stitches. It is useful for leaves and flower petals and gives an interesting texture. It should be worked with a straw needle.

Bring the needle through at the point where you wish to begin your stitch. Hold the thread below your work and insert the needle close to where the thread first emerged. Bring the needle out at the desired distance, as though you are making a small lazy daisy stitch, keeping the thread underneath. Do not pull the needle through at this stage. Wrap the thread around the needle three to five times (or desired number) in an anticlockwise direction. Place your left thumb over the wraps, then pull the needle and the thread firmly through the wraps. To anchor the stitch insert the needle at the tip of the bullion and pull through to the back of the fabric. Pass on to the beginning of the next stitch. Be sure to work each stitch the same to ensure that the long stitch down the side lies on the same side.

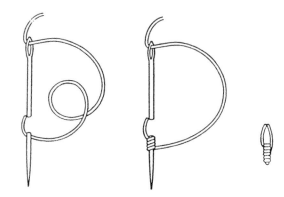

Lazy daisy bullion stitch

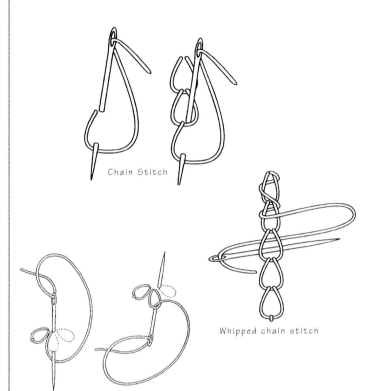

Chain Stitch

Whipped chain stitch

Lazy daisy or detached chain

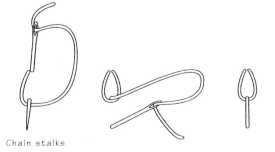

Chain stalks

CHAIN STITCH

Bring the needle through at the point where you wish to begin your chain stitch. Hold the thread below your work and insert the needle to the right, close to where the thread first emerged. Bring the needle out at the desired distance, keeping the thread underneath and draw up the stitch. Do not make the stitch too long or pull the chain too tight. The stitches should be even. Continue in this way working towards yourself along the design line.

WHIPPED CHAIN STITCH

This stitch is useful for stems. Work a row of chain stitch along the design line and bring the needle to the top of your work. With the blunt end of the needle whip back through each chain stitch, but not into the fabric.

LAZY DAISY OR DETACHED CHAIN

This is a very useful stitch for leaves and flower petals.

Bring the needle through at the point where you wish to begin your stitch. Hold the thread below your work and insert the needle to the right, close to where the thread first emerged. Bring the needle out at the desired distance, keeping the thread underneath. Fasten the loop at the end with a small straight stitch. Pass on to the beginning of the next stitch.

CHAIN STALKS

This stitch is worked as a lazy daisy stitch with the anchoring stitch extended to form a tail or stalk. For the Gazania and Arctotis leaves, work back to the stem rather than away from the stem.

DOUBLE LAZY DAISY STITCH OR BERRY STITCH

This stitch is useful for leaves, buds and flower petals. It can be worked in two colours.

The inside stitch is worked first as a lazy daisy stitch. The larger second stitch is worked outside and around the first stitch.

BUTTONHOLE STITCH

This stitch is the same as blanket stitch but the stitches are worked more closely together. It can be worked in a row or a circle.

Start on the outside edge and work from left to right. Hold the thread below and take a downward straight stitch and draw up with the thread underneath the needle. Continue in this way, spacing stitches as required.

FLY STITCH

Fly stitch is an open lazy daisy stitch. It can be worked either singly or collectivelly and arranged vertically or horizontally, or can radiate into a circle. The tying stitch can vary in length as required.

Bring the thread through at the top left of your design line. Insert the needle a little distance away to the right and take a small diagonal stitch to the centre with the thread below the needle. Pull through and fasten with a straight downward stitch.

Double lazy daisy stitch or berry stitch

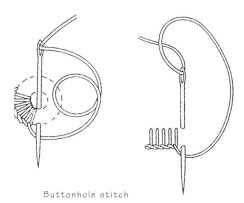

Buttonhole stitch

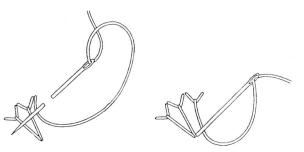

Fly stitch

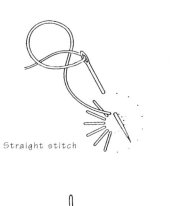

Straight stitch

Seeding

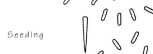

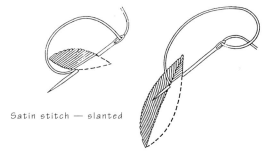

Satin stitch — slanted

STRAIGHT STITCH

Straight stitch is a single satin stitch and can be worked in any direction and to any length. The use of a small embroidery hoop will help you achieve good tension. Do not make the stitches too long as snagging may occur.

SEEDING

This is a simple filling stitch. Work tiny back stitches or straight stitches, of equal length in different directions, randomly over the area to be filled.

SATIN STITCH — SLANTED

This stitch should be worked with even stitches to cover the fabric completely, resulting in a smooth finish. To achieve good tension, use a small embroidery hoop and work with a stabbing motion.

A running stitch can be worked first to outline the design and will help to form a good edge. Work slanting stitches closely together across the outlined area.

LONG AND SHORT SATIN STITCH

This stitch can be used to fill areas too large to be covered by satin stitch. It can also be used to achieve subtle shading. The use of a small embroidery hoop will help you achieve good tension.

Work the first row in alternate long and short satin stitches. Closely follow the outline of the design shape. Work the following rows with long stitches in a brick fashion until the area is filled. Fill the gaps in the final row with short stitches.

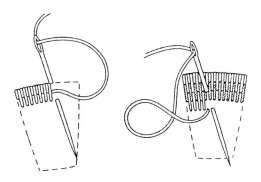

Long and short satin stitch

SATIN LEAF STITCH

This variation of satin stitch is easy to work and forms a very realistic leaf. It is taken from Brazilian embroidery.

The first stitch should be a little longer than you might expect, in order to form a good point on the leaf. Work the first satin stitch from the point of the leaf back into the centre of the leaf. Bring the needle back up on the right of the first stitch at the leaf tip. Take this second stitch back to the central leaf vein and insert the needle just below, but very close to the first stitch. Work the satin stitches alternately from each side fanning them as the leaf forms. At the same time, continue to work closely down the central vein. You may need to add one or two extra stitches on one side of your leaf if it is not symmetrical.

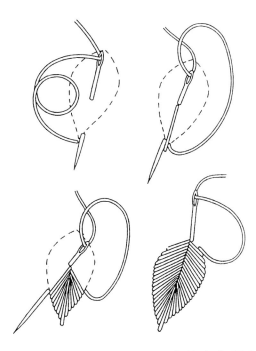

Satin leaf stitch

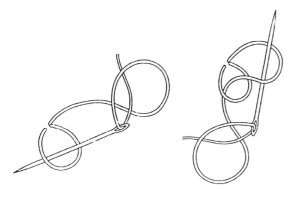

Starting and finishing

STARTING AND FINISHING

STARTING

❧ Start your embroidery with a couple of small running stitches or a back stitch under the area to be worked. You could use a knot, but it may show up when your finished piece is pressed.

FINISHING

Here are two satisfactory ways to finish off your thread:

❧ Finish as you started with a couple of running stitches or a back stitch under the area just worked.

❧ This method (illustrated) is used for smocking and is neat and secure. Take a small stitch to form a loop. Pass the needle through the loop to form a second loop. Pass the needle through the second loop and pull up tightly to form a secure knot.

❧ Finally, to neaten your work, weave the tag under your embroidery and cut off the end.

APPENDIX A

DMC STRANDED COTTON NUMBERS AND COLOUR NAMES USED IN *EMBROIDERY FROM THE GARDEN*

blanc neige		444	lemon — dark
ecru		445	lemon — light
209	lavender — dark	452	shell grey — medium
210	lavender — medium	469	avocado green
211	lavender — light	470	avocado green — light
223	shell pink — light	471	avocado green — very light
224	shell pink — very light	472	avocado green — ultra light
316	antique mauve — medium	522	fern green
320	pistachio green — medium	523	fern green — light
333	blue violet — very dark	524	fern green — very light
340	blue violet — medium	554	violet — light
341	blue violet — light	581	moss green
349	coral — dark	602	cranberry — medium
350	coral — medium	603	cranberry
351	coral	604	cranberry — light
352	coral — light	605	cranberry — very light
353	peach flesh	606	bright orange — red
356	terracotta — medium	611	drab brown — dark
369	pistachio green — very light	646	beaver grey — dark
371	mustard	718	plum
402	mahogany — very light	720	orange spice — dark

721	orange spice — medium	915	plum — dark	3348	yellow green — light
722	orange spice — light	938	coffee brown — ultra dark	3363	pine green — medium
725	topaz	946	burnt orange — medium	3364	pine green
726	topaz — light	972	canary — deep	3371	black brown
730	olive green — very dark	973	canary — bright	3607	plum — light
739	tan — ultra very light	977	golden brown — light	3609	plum — ultra light
741	tangerine — medium	3012	khaki green — medium	3689	mauve — light
742	tangerine — light	3013	khaki green — light	3721	shell pink — dark (red)
743	yellow — medium	3021	brown grey — very dark	3726	antique mauve — dark
745	yellow — light pale	3031	mocha brown — very dark	3733	dusty rose
746	off-white	3042	antique violet — very light	3740	antique violet — dark
778	antique mauve — very light	3051	green grey — dark	3746	blue violet — dark
783	topaz — medium	3052	green grey — medium	3772	nutmeg — light
791	cornflower blue — very dark	3053	green grey	3778	terracotta — light
792	cornflower blue — dark	3326	rose — light	3801	red — light
818	baby pink	3328	salmon — dark	3816	turquoise green
822	beige grey — light	3341	apricot	3823	yellow off-white
828	blue — ultra very light	3345	hunter green — dark	3830	terracotta — medium dark
841	beige brown — light	3346	hunter green		
898	coffee brown — very dark	3347	yellow green — medium		

APPENDIX B

THE FRAMING OF NEEDLEWORK

There are probably as many ways to frame a piece of needlework as there are ways to furnish a room in which the needlework will hang. While most will look attractive, few will be done correctly, and this will be revealed over a period of time.

The most important thing to remember in framing needlework, as indeed in framing any original artwork, is that the nature of the work should not be materially altered during the framing process. In the case of recently completed needlework of the size referred to in this book, this means that, before the embroidery is placed in the frame, it should be laced over archivally sound board in the manner illustrated (see illustration 1). This will keep it firm and straight inside the frame. Your picture framer should be able to supply you with the correct grade of card on which to lace the embroidery.

It should not be glued down with wet glue or dry mounted in a heat press. Both these methods will cause the fabric to discolour and hasten its deterioration. Neither is it recommended that needlework be stapled on to a backing board or kept in position with masking tape.

Many embroiderers prefer to do the lacing of the work themselves. It is not difficult, merely time-consuming and, therefore, expensive if a professional carries out the operation. Care must be taken to ensure that the weave of the fabric is straight and that the embroidery remains clean. Remember that grease transferred from hands to the surface of the fabric may not show up immediately, but will become apparent in time.

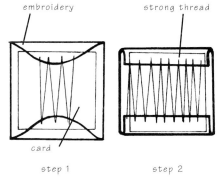

step 1   step 2

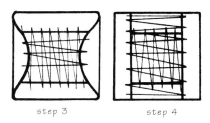

step 3   step 4

Illustration 1
Lacing an embroidery — from the back

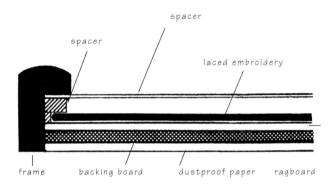

Illustration 2
Framing without a matt—side view

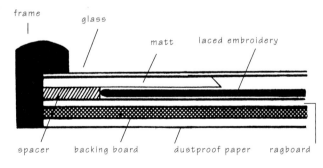

Illustration 3
Framing with a matt—side view

Having laced the needlework on to its backing, it is ready for framing.

Decisions will now have to be made on what sort of frame best suits the embroidery, whether or not it should be placed behind glass, and if it should be 'matted' with a cardboard surround. These are not only aesthetic considerations but also very practical ones.

On cottage embroidery, simple wooden frames, with maybe just a hint of colour along the inside edge, work best. More complicated frames, particularly gilt ones, tend to overwhelm the needlework. Whatever frame is chosen, it should be deep enough and strong enough to accommodate the embroidery, the glass, the backing and any other materials used.

As a general rule, embroideries are best put behind glass. Glazing keeps the dust off, prevents them becoming dirty, and will help keep the silverfish out. However, when the work is glazed, care should be taken that the glass does not touch the surface of the embroidery: moisture condensing on the inside of the glass can migrate into the fabric and cause the fibres to deteriorate. Glass can be kept away from the embroidery either with a small spacer placed between the glass and the embroidery, underneath the rebate of the frame (see illustration 2), or by using a single or double matt (see illustration 3), or a combination of spacer and matt if the surface of the embroidery is raised.

Because the needlework and the glass are separated, non-glare or non-reflective glass should not be used. Most non-glare glass when used in this way blurs the image and dulls the colour. Clear glass is required or, if the embroidery is to hang in a very brightly lit area, a Plexiglas which inhibits the passage of ultra-violet light should be considered.

Except on samplers, matting is recommended as it is not only practical but also serves a very important aesthetic function. An archivally sound, coloured matt (green is often used when the image contains flowers) will not only enhance the image but also prevent the frame from visually crowding the embroidery. Remember that matts look better if they are large — at least five centimetres (2 inches) wide, with the bottom of the matt, slightly larger than the top and the sides, say six or seven centimetres (2 1/2 - 3 inches). Any smaller than this and the matt and frame may look like concentric, coloured rectangles around the image, and the whole effect will be spoiled.

It is important that the card on which the embroidery is laced, and that used for the matting and backing of the embroidery, is archivally sound. Normal wood-pulp card is not archivally sound. It contains acidic materials which will eventually mark the embroidery.

Finally, when the embroidery is placed in the frame, the frame should be sealed with a good quality tape (not masking tape as it deteriorates too quickly) or completely papered over. This will prevent any dust or insect life entering the frame from the back.

If you adhere to these basic principles this should ensure the long life of the embroidery.

Ross Henty
Canberra Art Framing Company

INDEX
THE FLOWER GLOSSARY

INDEX
THE STITCH GLOSSARY

BIBLIOGRAPHY

Bulbs for all Climates. (Series:The Australian Women's Weekly Garden Guides)
ACP Publishing Pty Ltd, Sydney, 1994.

Lampe, D. *More Embroidered Garden Flowers.* Sally Milner Publishing Pty Ltd, Burra
Creek, NSW, 1993.

Macoboy, S. *Stirling Macoboy's What Flower is That?* Weldon Publishing, Sydney,
NSW, 1986.

Mann, R. *The Ultimate Book of Flowers for Australian Gardens.* Random House
(Australia) Pty Ltd, 1995.

Pienaar, K. *The South African What Flower is That?* Struik Publishers (Pty) Ltd, Cape
Town, 1984.

Pienaar, K. *Gardening with Indigenous Plants.* Struik Publishers (Pty) Ltd, Cape
Town, 1991.

Tootill, E. (ed.) *The Penguin Dictionary of Botany.* Penguin Books Ltd,
Harmondsworth, Middlesex, 1984.

Wild Flowers of South Africa. Struik Publishers (Pty) Ltd, Cape Town, 1980.